RAY WATKINSON – WILLIAM MORRIS AS DESIGNER

La Belle Iseult William Morris's only known easel picture, painted in 1858 in Oxford, with Jane Burden as model *Tate Gallery, London*

RAY WATKINSON

William Morris as Designer

Trefoil Publications

Published by
Trefoil Publications Ltd
7 Royal Parade, Dawes Road,
London SW6

British Library Cataloguing in Publication Date
Watkinson, Raymond
William Morris as designer — 2nd ed

1. Design. English. Morris, William, 1834-1896
I. Title
745.4'493

ISBN 0 86294 040 0

Printed and bound in Portugal

Contents

Illustrations

Acknowledgements

In acknowledging all the help I have had from friends and strangers alike while working on this book. I must reserve to myself all blame for its shortcomings. I wish to record thanks to the following for help, particularly in respect of illustrative material:

To members of the staff of the Victoria and Albert Museum, with especial thanks to Mrs Barbara Morris; to members of the staff of the William Morris Gallery, Walthamstow; to the City Art Gallery, Birmingham; to Messrs Sandersons for access to material and photographs of records; to Messrs George Newnes – *Country Life*; to the Rector of Middleton Cheney; to the Vicar of St Margaret's, Rottingdean; to the Vicar of St Michael and All Angels, Brighton; to Mr Robin Carruthers. For particular help with photographs, often at very short notice: Mrs Susan Keep of the Victoria and Albert Museum; Mr Dennis Frone; Mrs Jasmine Thorpe; Mr W. V. Whittaker and Mr Tom Buckeridge, of the Brighton College of Art; and to all other colleagues at Brighton for their generous and friendly interest; to the staff of Studio Vista, of course, for their patience.

Introduction

William Morris did more than design the finest wallpapers and fabrics of the nineteenth century, master half a dozen crafts, and write some of the finest poetry of his age. He belongs to our own time as much as to his, and nobody of his time is more worth the trouble of re-examination.

The object of heroic admiration, he had first become famous as a poet in the 1860s with *The Earthly Paradise*; for the next thirty years he exercised a growing influence on the practice of design and the revival of crafts. His ideas on the nature of art and its function in society stretched from Ruskin to Marx. 'We should have nothing in our houses,' he said, 'which we did not either know to be useful or believe to be beautiful.' Art he called 'the expression of man's delight in his labour, a joy to the maker and the user'; but art could only be this on the condition of social equality: it must be for all; a necessary part of the great human birthright – or it would die.

He has been generally presented as a backward-looking simple-lifer, out of touch with the realities of human progress. Stylistically, nothing could be further from his own productions than the rational functionalism of the twentieth century. Yet Walter Gropius, head of the famous Bauhaus from which so much of modern thought and form emerged in the 1920s and early 1930s, wrote in his *The New Architecture and the Bauhaus* – 'Ruskin and Morris strove to find a means of reuniting the world of art with the world of work. Towards the end of the century their lead was followed by Van de Velde, Olbrich, Behrens and others on the Continent.'

It was Van de Velde, admirer of Morris, who was first head of the Bauhaus, and when he retired recommended Gropius, another admirer, to succeed him. Muthesius, adviser on education for art and design to the Prussian Government, spent some years in England studying the Arts and Crafts Movement which so largely sprang from Morris's work. However much style may have changed, the thread runs unbroken from Morris to our own time.

At sight, the proposition that the severe forms of twentieth-century design owe anything to Morris may seem absurd. How could this lover of Gothic, disciple of Ruskin, begetter of the Arts and Crafts Movement, hater of factory production, be also the forerunner of the new architecture, the new industrial design, and the new typography?

If we have looked only at style, the contradiction may well prove absolute. But if we look deeper, find out what Morris really did, on what principles he worked, how his thought developed; if we realise that to him 'function' related always to human life and activity, never just to the mechanism, form, or material of particular objects, the contradiction dissolves. It was Morris's historical understanding of what he was doing, that made him so potent a force.

Three musicians designed by Edward Burne-Jones was engraved by Morris and appears on the title-page of *The Earthly Paradise*. It seems to derive from one of Burne-Jones's earlier designs for the abandoned illustrated *Earthly Paradise*

'Enter Love, disguised as a maker of pictured cloths.' – LOVE IS ENOUGH

1 Life and background

William Morris was born on March 24, 1834, at Elm House, Clay Hill, Walthamstow, on London's north-eastern fringe. In the 1830s, Walthamstow was in effect the country; or sufficiently nearly so to make it attractive to business men who could afford to move out of town. This was exactly the situation of William Morris senior. Born in Worcester in 1797, of Welsh descent, he had come to London as a young man and entered the Quaker house of Harris, Sanderson and Harris, bill and discount brokers, in which he became a partner. Marrying Emma Shelton, daughter of a Worcester music teacher, he set up house, in the old mercantile tradition, over the firm's premises in Lombard Street. Here two daughters were born, and then, in 1833, the family moved to Walthamstow where William Morris, 'poet, artist, manufacturer and socialist', was born.

The business prospered, and the family moved again in 1840 to Woodford Hall. The new home was a large Georgian house, on the very edge of Epping Forest, set in a small park and surrounded by its own farmland on the banks of the River Roding. William Morris, the elder, obtained a grant of arms from the College of Heralds in 1843; and the life of the household was much more like that of a country gentleman than of the city business man which, after all, he continued to be.

A year later, when the Devon Great Consols Company was formed to exploit new copper-mines in Cornwall and Devon, his income began to be very much increased. Expanding engineering industries needed copper; production swelled; the value of the company's shares, of which Morris owned roughly one-quarter, rocketed within six months to 800 times their initial value, and his holding was worth more than £200,000. The income from this handsome investment was added to that from the business which had already enabled him to establish himself at Woodford, in the best English tradition, as a quasi-squire. When he died, in 1847, he left a substantial fortune. It would be difficult to say what it would be worth in mid-twentieth-century terms, but it was large enough for him not only to provide for his widow and younger children, but to leave William, the eldest son, an income of £900 a year on his coming of age, little of which would be drawn off by taxation. We might multiply the figure by ten to suggest what sort of income Morris commanded during most of his university career. It was, at all events, far beyond that of any of the young men with whom he became friendly at Oxford.

Most of these young men came from Birmingham, and were familiar with the grim industrial scene from which his own life had been so remote. An unearned income on such a scale must have become a monstrous reproach to his tender conscience as he talked with these new friends, and as with them he read Carlyle, Kingsley, and Ruskin. But before Oxford came schooldays, spent at Marlborough College.

At Marlborough there was little order, and much unorganised leisure; but there was a considerable library which catered to his growing passion for architecture and history, while he spent his leisure in exploring the surrounding country, its churches and monuments, including the ancient mysterious circle of Avebury. An energetic and restless boy who had to be always doing or making, he also had developed early a habit of concentrated reading which enabled him to absorb and retain an unusual fund of knowledge that was not only architectural. As a result, one of the comments of a new acquaintance when he went up to Oxford was 'how he seemed to know things'.

The Morris family was Evangelical; but Marlborough had been founded by high churchmen. The chapel, still building when Morris joined the school, was designed by Edward Blore, architect of Sir Walter Scott's house at Abbotsford; and the choir played an important part in the life of the school. One of Morris's letters to Emma (April 13, 1849) describes explorations of the countryside and visits to Avebury and Silbury; but it opens with a long passage describing the singing of the anthem on Easter Sunday. Religious ideas not yet disturbed, romantic relish of the past, and aesthetic responses to building and ritual all drew Morris towards the high church, as they had done many others. The influence of the Ecclesiologists and the Tractarians, Pugin's vision of an England renewed in glorious Gothic and Catholic worship and architecture, the handsome albums of engravings of mediaeval monuments, learned books by men like Thomas Rickman and Henry Shaw on the buildings, the art, costume and illuminated books of the Middle Ages, the mediaevalism of the Waverley novels – all this moved young men of Morris's generation towards a high Anglican position, and often into the Roman Church. His mother's family had associations with the Cathedral of Worcester, where her grandfather had been a diocesan official, and her uncle a minor canon: the choral tradition of church music, rather than secular music, always had a special appeal for Morris; and clearly religion meant a great deal to his mother. It was natural for him and his family to assume the Church as his vocation, rather than necessary for any anxious decision to be made that he should take orders.

A feature of English society in the mid nineteenth century was the setting up of schools whose function was to train the sons of the rising middle class to rule in industry, which was the foundation of their social and political being, and to rule in Parliament (now, since the Reform Act of 1832, an institution in which they had a direct voice and could wield new power). Rugby School under Dr Arnold's direction is the classic example; but there were new foundations too, of which Marlborough was one. The high principles, the healthy and convenient situation, could not by themselves bring into being the kind of school which the founders, and the parents of the boys, wanted. In 1851 there was an organised mutiny; one consequence of which was that Morris did not return after the Christmas vacation, but spent the next six months in private study with the Rev. F. B. Guy, an assistant master at the Forest School in Walthamstow, who also coached young men for the universities.

Morris seems to have had little formal instruction at Marlborough, where lack of space and lack of organisation alike militated against it; but he spent the whole of the year 1852 under Guy's tuition; for though he matriculated in June of that year at Exeter College, Oxford was then so full that he could not take up his place until 1853. When he went up, it was with the intention of taking holy orders.

In 1850 his sister Emma had married the curate of Downe, in Kent – the Rev. Joseph Oldham, a high churchman, though the Morris family was itself Evangelical. Emma had always been the closest to Morris of the whole family, and in their letters during his schooldays they exchanged not only family gossip, but thoughts about the Church, its music, its architecture. An interest in Gothic architecture, part-romantic, part-devotional, pervaded English middle-class thought in the first half of the nineteenth century to an extent now difficult to realise. Eighteenth-century antiquarianism and pursuit of the picturesque, the love of Gothic orna-ment as an exotic, had given way to a more serious and orderly inquiry into structure and development. Alongside the purely decorative values, religious and ethical values also informed the curiosity about what was now thought of as England's own especial form of architecture. It was at the same time an object of curiosity and national pride in Germany and France; but the idea of Gothic as international was acceptable only to Roman Catholics or those with Roman leanings: to most others Gothic was the English style.

At the same time, the Gothic novel had by no means run its course; Mrs Radcliffe, 'Monk' Lewis, Clara Reeve, were still reprinted and widely read, while Scott had raised certain elements of the genre to a much higher level. William and Emma Morris, reading such romances as Clara Reeve's *Old English Baron* in the park at Woodford and hurrying home in terror in the dusk, were not exceptional in their taste for mediaeval romance. Morris's father must have shared it. Morris went with him as a little boy to visit old churches, and was once taken as far as Canterbury; which left so deep an impression on him that to the end of his life he could visualise and describe the cathedral.

When he went up to matriculate in the summer of 1852, he had sat next to another young man; whether Morris had noticed him or not, this tall, pale boy from Birmingham had been struck by him, had seen him, in the morning, fold up his Horace paper and write William Morris on it in his firm, legible hand. Now, though Edward Jones's own Birmingham school-mates were mostly at Pembroke, these two strangers very quickly became inseparable friends and companions. Exeter was so full that it was not until the autumn that there were rooms available for freshmen, who had to lodge out of college. This, the inadequacy of the teaching, and the attractions of old friends at Pembroke, drew Burne-Jones, and with him Morris, into a group outside Exeter, most of them from Birmingham. Even when they moved into rooms in their own college, Morris and Jones still moved in 'the Set' – Fulford, Dixon, Faulkner,

Cornell Price, Macdonald. 'Within, and yet above or apart from the rest of this group,' says Mackail, 'the two Exeter undergraduates lived in undivided intimacy and unremitting intellectual tension.'

They read, and talked, enormously. Much of their reading was theological, for Jones also intended to enter the Church. But a great deal was history and poetry – Morris was already an admirer of Tennyson, and of Ruskin's *Modern Painters*, two volumes of which had appeared. Keats, Shelley, Carlyle, Kingsley, Thackeray, Dickens, Thorpe's *Northern Mythology*, Charlotte Yonge's *The Heir of Redclyffe*, La Motte Fouqué's *Sintram*, were all admired and discussed. But Morris's intellectual life was not then or ever confined to the world of books. Oxford itself, as a town, played an incalculable part in developing his ideas. In spite of the recent intrusion of the railway, the city still looked mediaeval in aspect: Morris and Burne-Jones both described it in later life as they had then known it. 'On all sides,' Burne-Jones wrote, 'except where it touched the railway, the city ended abruptly, as if a wall had been about it, and you came suddenly upon the meadows. There was little brick in the city, it was either grey with stone or yellow with the wash of the pebble-dash in the poorer streets. It was an endless delight to us to wander about the streets, where were still many old houses with wood carving and a little sculpture here and there. The Chapel of Merton College had been lately renovated by Butterfield, and Pollen, a former Fellow of Merton, had painted the roof of it. Many an afternoon we spent in that chapel. Indeed I think the buildings of Merton and the Cloisters of New College were our chief shrines in Oxford.'

Morris's interests were by no means wholly in the past, however much the past might colour the present. Painted decoration, coloured encaustic tiles, stained glass – however deplorable much might be in conception – were all part of the stirring of the new ideas, which, bound up with religious movements and church architecture and furnishing, were felt in secular building, decoration, and furniture. Morris subscribed to *The Builder*, as well as studying manuscripts in the Bodleian and the newest sets of engravings after Giotto, Van Eyck, Fra Angelico, issued by the Arundel Society. From the Turl, almost opposite to Exeter College, John Henry Parker published his handsomely illustrated volumes on Gothic architecture – Rickman's then definitive work; his own book on *Fourteenth Century Domestic Architecture;* Charles Winston's anonymous, authoritative book on *Ancient Glass* – books on a past whose forms were daily being applied to new buildings by such original architects as Butterfield and Street.

It was their love of the arts that held the Set together, more than their formal studies; and for Morris, at this point, though he had begun to write poetry this meant architecture above all. His vacations were spent in visiting churches and making brass rubbings; in 1854 he first travelled abroad, to visit France and Belgium, seeing Rouen, Chartres, Beauvais, Amiens, and Paris. In the summer months following he began to write prose romances, and read Chaucer with Burne-Jones. During this summer too he, Burne-Jones, and Fulford made a month's tour in northern France, Morris acting as guide to his own discoveries of the previous year. Writing to Cornell Price from Avranches in August, he tells how they have seen nine cathedrals and twenty-four 'splendid churches; some of them surpassing first-rate English cathedrals'. At the end of this journey Morris made up his mind not to enter the Church, but to become an architect. Burne-Jones made a similar resolve to devote himself to painting.

They had by now discovered the Pre-Raphaelites. Painting took on a new meaning for them. They first learned of these painters by reading Ruskin's *Edinburgh Lectures*. Then Millais's *Return of the Dove to the Ark* had been exhibited in Wyatt's shop in the High; and in the summer of 1854, at the Royal Academy, Burne-Jones had seen Hunt's *The Awakened Conscience* and *The Light of the World*. In May 1855 Morris and Burne-Jones had gone to see the Pre-Raphaelite paintings in Windus's Collection – including Ford Madox Brown's *The Last of England*; a little later they saw paintings by Hunt and Rossetti in the house of Mr Combe, head of the Clarendon Press. They had also, by now, seen a copy of *The Germ*; and Rossetti became a special source of inspiration to them.

In Morris's last term at Oxford he worked for his finals and negotiated with G. E. Street, whose office was then in Oxford, to take up articles with him. He also set about making and engraving illustrations inspired by Rossetti's drawing for William Allingham's *Day and Night Songs*. Rossetti was 'of all men on earth, the one' whom Burne-Jones now wished to meet. This he did at Christmas, at the Workingmen's College in Great Ormond Street, 'where men skilled in science or history gave lectures or their services of evenings', and where Rossetti, Madox Brown, and John Ruskin himself gave lessons in drawing.

In January 1856, Morris met Philip Webb, then Street's chief clerk, who became his life-long friend and collaborator. Working for Street, he was still able to meet daily with all his friends – except Burne-Jones, who had gone to learn under Rossetti to be a painter, and Fulford, who, as Editor of *The Oxford and Cambridge Magazine* which they had just launched, had also gone to London. He was prepared to underwrite the venture to the tune of some hundreds of pounds a year. It was in this journal that Morris's first published work appeared: several prose stories, some poems, an account of the Cathedral of Amiens, and reviews of Browning's *Men and Women* and of Rethel's woodcuts then just published.

Outside his work in Street's office, Morris began to work in calligraphy and illumination, in modelling and carving, as well as writing poems and romances. At weekends he would visit Burne-Jones in London, and so met Rossetti, who had a profound influence on him; profound and unique, for to no other personality did Morris ever submit his own as he did, for a while, to Rossetti.

This pattern continued during the first six months of 1856. Morris was drawn more and more into the Rossetti circle, meeting Ford Madox Brown and Holman Hunt; he was buying paintings – Arthur Hughes's *April Love*, and Ford Madox Brown's *Hayfield*, and being more and more persuaded by Rossetti that he too should paint. 'Rossetti says I ought to paint, he says I shall be able; now as he is a very great man, and speaks with authority, and not as the scribes, I must try. So I am going to try, not giving up the architecture, but trying if it is possible to get six hours a day for drawing besides office work.' Even for a man of Morris's enormous energy, this suggests an effort difficult to sustain. But it became possible because Street moved his office to London that summer. Burne-Jones and Morris lived in rooms near by, and both went to life classes in the evenings. But later in the year, while in Belgium with Street, who had entered designs for the new Hôtel de Ville of Lille, Morris saw again the Flemish paintings which had so moved him on his first trip abroad, and came back decided to abandon architecture in favour of painting.

He did this with a good deal of self-doubt; his drawing, he knew, was weak; he was already twenty-three, and had already abandoned his first intention – that of taking orders. It was not an easy decision, and probably only the intense pressure of Rossetti's personality made it seem possible.

The attempt to become a painter lasted from late 1856 to early 1859, during which period Morris and Burne-Jones lived in rooms at 17 Red Lion Square, where Rossetti and Deverell had formerly been tenants. As the rooms were unfurnished, Morris set to work to design furniture for them. It would be a mistake to think of these designs as being consciously directed to the reform of taste. They were made to meet private need and satisfy personal taste; and in what he did, Morris, far from being an innovator, was following a pattern well-set in the profession he had just abandoned and in the one he had just taken up. Architects like Owen Jones, Digby Wyatt, Butterfield, and Burges had all designed chairs, tables, cabinets, some of which had been shown in the Great Exhibition of 1851. An important difference between these and Morris's Red Lion Square pieces was the innocence of the latter; the famous settle, for instance, was a very plain object, with none of the Gothic quirks to be seen in pieces by Burges or Pugin. It was not conceived as the challenge to public taste which it has since been imagined to be, but as a purely utilitarian object. The fact that it was forthwith enriched by Rossetti's paintings of *Love between the Sun and the Moon*, and of *The Meeting of Dante and Beatrice* does not alter this, though it made the settle a model for subsequent designs in which similar paintings were incorporated (as in the great wardrobe, and the cupboard which still stands in the hall of the Red House).

The Red House was a landmark in Morris's life, though not the landmark in architecture which it has been thought. Like the furniture – both that designed for Red Lion Square and that for the new house, the Red House itself fits naturally into the pattern of thought and design of the sort of architect with whom Morris had worked, and which he would have become had he stayed in the profession. A harsh red-brick style had already been set for a number of domestic Gothic buildings, such as parsonages and country schools. Webb, the designer of the Red House, worked naturally enough in this vein.

The occasion of the building of the house was, of course, Morris's marriage to Jane Burden; and this itself was perhaps the most momentous outcome of one of Rossetti's ambitious schemes.

Early in the summer of 1857 Rossetti projected a scheme for the decoration of the new Union Debating Hall in Oxford, which his friend the architect Benjamin Woodward had designed and which was nearing completion. On its open timber roof, and on the wall immediately below, Rossetti suggested, paintings could be carried out. The scheme was accepted. Rossetti hurried back to London to enlist helpers – Burne-Jones, Morris, Arthur Hughes, Spencer Stanhope, Val Prinsep, and Hungerford Pollen who had already, though an amateur, done some decorative painting on the roof of Merton College Chapel. But none of them had any idea of the technical problems of the work to which Rossetti was committing them – certainly Rossetti had not. There was talk of fresco – a splendid word; but what they did was to paint, in distemper, on still damp walls, decorations which within six months were fading, though Coventry Patmore described them at the end of 1857 as 'so brilliant as to make the walls look like the margin of an illuminated manuscript'.

At the end of 1857 the work was abandoned; Rossetti, Burne-Jones, Prinsep, and Hughes all returned to London, with a fine irresponsibility. Morris stayed in Oxford, drawing, painting, carving, studying embroidery, and writing a great deal of poetry; but, above all, pursuing his courtship of Jane Burden. Sixteen-year-old Jane had been discovered at the theatre one evening; persuaded to sit for Rossetti, she had spent much time with the painters, listening to their serious discussions, posing as queens and princesses, taking part in their very jolly amusements.

In March 1858, Morris's first volume of poems, *The Defence of Guenevere*, appeared, published by Bell and Daldy (perhaps on Street's recommendation, since in the same year they published his book on the Scudamore Organs). About the same time, Morris was at work on a painting commissioned – through Rossetti, of course – by Plint of Leeds. In the summer, with Faulkner and Philip Webb, he revisited France, rowing down the Seine from Paris, discussing the house he would build when he married Jane the following year. His preoccupation with Jane and marriage no doubt helped to free him from the tensions and moods of doubt which had beset him since leaving Street's office; and perhaps also freed him from Rossetti's domination. Without, apparently, ever making any formal decision to abandon painting, such as had marked the change from Church to architecture and from architecture to painting, he became so involved, during the months of planning and furnishing the new house, that easel painting passed out of his work for good.

He was married in April 1859, and after a six weeks' honeymoon on the Continent the couple came back to rooms in London. Burne-Jones abandoned Red Lion Square for Charlotte Street, and the furniture which Rossetti had described as 'incubi and succubi' was moved to the new house at Bexleyheath, Kent, in the summer of 1860. Webb had designed some new furniture, table glass, candlesticks of copper, and other furnishings. No wallpapers brightened – or darkened – the new walls. They, and the ceilings, were to be decorated in part with painted patterns, in part pictorially, in part with hangings embroidered by Janey and Georgiana Burne-Jones; Janey's sister, Bessie, and Kate Faulkner, sister of Charles. Around the house, which stood in an orchard, a garden as mediaeval as the paintings was planned, with long walks and trellis-enclosed flower plots. The decoration and furnishing became an enterprise in which all Morris's friends seemed to be continually engaged. In a mixture of hard work and picnic, they set about turning the Red House into 'the beautifullest house in the world' as Burne-Jones called it.

Morris disliked almost everything that could be bought ready made; but there can be no doubt that the positive stimulus of planning, making, designing, seeing the place grow, was more important to him than his dislike of the shop article. His own expressions of distaste at the then available furniture, papers, hangings, and over-romantic ideas about his life, have meant that too much emphasis has been placed on negative motives, hiding the fact that he was doing, in his own very different way, what Pugin had done years before at Salisbury and Ramsgate, when he designed and furnished his two houses.

Out of the Red House came the idea of an association of artists for the design and making of better furniture and furnishings. Like the idea of the house itself, this was not new. All the friends had been members of the Hogarth Club; Rossetti had been one of the Pre-Raphaelite Brethren, Madox Brown and Hughes close associates; the Pembroke Set at Oxford had always been on the point of establishing some more formal community. The idea of association was familiar; and there was the direct precedent of 'Felix Summerly's Art Manufactures'.

In one important respect the association now proposed seemed to take a step back. No thought seems to have been given to the nature of industrial production; quite simply, a group of painters and a couple of civil engineers banded together to make, on a craft basis, with the help of their wives and sisters, every kind of domestic, or church, furniture. It was a very amateurish affair, and might well have petered out, as the enthusiastic associations of young people are apt to do. But, between them, they had sufficient connections in the architectural profession to bring in commissioned work which introduced its own discipline; and Morris had at last found a channel through which all his interests and energies could flow. The wealth which had seemed likely to make him a dilettante freed him to undertake what none of the others could, the general management of their affairs.

The firm of Morris, Marshall, Faulkner and Company issued its prospectus in April 1861. This document, which has all the marks of Rossetti's style, reads as follows:

Morris, Marshall, Faulkner and Company, Fine Art Workmen in Painting, Carving, Furniture and the Metals.

The growth of Decorative Art in this country owing to the effort of English Architects has now reached a point at which it seems desirable that Artists of reputation should devote their time to it. Although no doubt particular instances of success may be cited, still it must be generally felt that attempts of this kind hitherto have been crude and fragmentary. Up to this time want of artistic supervision, which can alone bring about harmony between the various parts of a successful work, has been increased by the necessarily excessive outlay consequent on taking one individual artist from his pictorial labour.

The Artists whose names appear above hope by association to do away with this difficulty. Having among their numbers men of varied qualifications, they will be able to undertake any species of decoration, mural or otherwise, from pictures, properly so called, down to the consideration of the smallest work susceptible of art beauty. It is anticipated that by such co-operation, the largest amount of what is essentially the artist's work, along with his constant supervision, will be secured at the smallest possible expense, while the work must necessarily be of a much more complete order, than if any single artist were incidentally employed in the usual manner.

These artists having been for many years deeply attached to the study of the Decorative Arts of all time and countries, have felt more than most people the want of some one place, where they could either obtain or get produced work of a genuine and beautiful character. They have therefore now established themselves as a firm, for the production, by themselves and under their supervision of –

i   Mural Decoration, either in Pictures or in Pattern work, or merely in the arrangement of colours, as applied to dwelling houses, churches, or public buildings.
ii   Carving generally, as applied to Architecture.
iii   Stained Glass, especially with reference to its harmony with Mural Decoration.
iv   Metal Work in all its branches, including Jewellery.
v   Furniture, either depending for its beauty on its own design, on the application of materials hitherto overlooked, or on its conjunction with Figure and Pattern Painting. Under this head is included Embroidery of all kinds, Stamped Leather, and ornamental work in other such materials, besides every article necessary for domestic use.

It is only requisite to state further, that work of all the above classes will be estimated for and executed in a business-like manner; and it is believed that good decoration, involving rather the luxury of taste than the luxury of costliness, will be found to be much less expensive than is generally supposed.

April 11, 1861

The work which had gone on spontaneously before could not, now it had put on a public face, be carried on successfully without London premises. These were found in Red Lion Square. Commissions came chiefly from architects like Bodley, who was at work on two new churches: one at Scarborough (St Martin's) and one at Brighton (St Michael's). Ford Madox Brown, Rossetti, and Burne-Jones had designed stained glass for Powell of Whitefriars from 1856 onwards, and glass, painted woodwork, altar cloths, and other church furnishings formed the basis of the firm's work. There was a good deal of new church building afoot which brought a steady flow of such work; but there were domestic commissions too, some on a substantial scale like that for decorations in the new house which Birket Foster, the watercolourist, had just built at Witley in Surrey.

Morris, though he had no more responsibility as a designer than anybody else, was manager, at a salary of £150; Faulkner, at the same salary, business manager and book-keeper. The firm's capital was tiny: £1 per share from each of the partners, and a loan of £100 from Morris's mother launched them on their first year's work.

The firm began as a kind of artists' co-operative, but it was hardly surprising that in the end it should become a business which Morris managed and owned. Already, in April 1861, at the very moment of the firm's launching, he was thinking in these terms. His letter to his old tutor, Guy, which was sent with a copy of the firm's circular, and asked for Guy's help in finding clients, makes this clear:

'My dear Guy,
        By reading the enclosed you will see that I have started as a decorator which I have long meant to do when I could get men of reputation to join me, and to this end mainly I have built my fine house.'

What sort of reaction this would have provoked from Madox Brown or Rossetti, had they seen it, makes interesting speculation; and Jane Morris might have thought that there were other reasons for building the house. Morris was exercising some licence making such a statement; and yet in the preceding five or six years he and his friends must often have discussed just this sort of thing. The essential meaning of this statement is surely that he had at last found his way.

He threw himself energetically into the work: designing, making, selling, experimenting with materials, travelling to advise on the decoration of churches and houses, working out schemes, making estimates.

Stained glass was the most important part of their work for some years; but the first articles actually sold were some pieces of table glass, designed by Webb and made by Powell. Jewellery, furniture, embroideries, and hangings were made and sold. Tiles and wallpapers followed; the latter designed by Morris, who now, released from the problems of painting, found his real gifts as a designer of flat pattern. The first designed wallpapers were rather old-fashioned and naturalistic; very different from the geometric austerities being produced by men like Owen Jones. By the end of 1862 the firm had begun to establish itself, and had won two medals at the Great Exhibition, with stained glass, furniture, and mediaeval-mannered hangings embroidered after Morris's designs. Tiles sent had been discreetly withheld from actual exhibition when they discovered that William Burges, one of the judges, did not like them. Not only did they win medals; they sold nearly £150 worth of goods.

The Red House, matrix of all this endeavour, still occupied the friends; additions were to enclose a big quadrangle, and in the new half of the house Burne-Jones and his Georgiana would live. Morris's two daughters were born here – Jane (Jenny) in 1861 and Mary (May) in 1862. But the demands of the business grew, and in 1864 Morris had a severe illness. The joint household and the little colony of workshops were abandoned. The 'most beautiful house in England' was, with real grief, given up for an old house in Queen Square, Bloomsbury; Morris and his family never saw it again.

---

2 The firm

During the years at Upton, Morris had written little poetry, though a great cycle of poems was planned of which a scheme survives – *Scenes from the Fall of Troy*. The Trojan story had been the basis of the painted decorations at the Red House; it dated from the years of *Guenevere*. In the first-drafted fragments, the direct and luminous imagery, simple language, and mediaeval assumptions of *Guenevere*, as well as the brutal drama not found anywhere else in Morris's poems, make a marked contrast with the *Life and Death of Jason*, published in 1867.

But in 1865 Morris was wholly taken up with the firm, translating it to Queen Square, and converting part of the house there into workshops. Although the other partners continued to design, Morris was by now in full charge. Effectively, Morris was the firm. The business side was taken over by Warington Taylor, who managed the firm with a strong hand and swept it clean of amateurism. In the five years until his death in 1870, his careful management released Morris to spend all his energies on the design side and stabilised the concern in a way which its originators could not have done. During this period two important commissions came to the firm; the decoration of the Green Dining Room at the new Victoria and Albert Museum, and the decoration of a suite of rooms at St James's Palace. Both schemes have survived, although that at St James's has been modified and the Green Dining Room is no longer used as a dining-room; it is now the William Morris Room, used to display furniture and fabrics produced by the firm.

The changing situation released Morris to write poetry again, and he began the long cycle called *The Earthly Paradise*, in 1866, the first volume of which appeared in 1868. On the title-page of this volume was an engraving by Morris from a design by Burne-Jones of three women musicians. The publisher was F. S. Ellis.

In the same year, Morris began to study Icelandic with Erikr Magnusson. He had known something of the sagas since Oxford days; now he began to read them in the original with

Magnusson, and to publish translations; the first appeared early in 1869. During the summer, Jane Morris's health began to break, and they spent two months at the German spa of Ems. Most of *The Earthly Paradise* was now finished. The last volume appeared in 1870; as did the translation of *The Volsunga Saga* – for Morris the most moving of all ancient stories. The firm had become less exigent; it had more momentum and more expert hands. Morris now found time to draw and paint again; but, more significantly in terms of creative work, he resumed his calligraphy, beginning by writing out and illuminating for Georgiana Burne-Jones a volume of his own poems.

Now thirty-six, he was established as a designer, and highly respected as a poet. In 1869 Watts painted his portrait, one of the series he was devoting to the great men of the age. Morris was now looking for a house out of London, partly because he was in some respects freer from the daily demands of the business, but also because of a crisis in his marriage. The late 1860s were a time of stress, however languorous the poems of *The Earthly Paradise* may be. Early in 1871, he came across Kelmscott Manor, near Lechlade, which he visited a second time, with Rossetti, with whom he proposed to share it, and with Janey, with whom Rossetti was by now deeply in love. Morris's own description of the house in *News from Nowhere* is not likely to be bettered by any other. Kelmscott is a typical stone house of the Upper Thames Valley, built in a style which lingered long after the fifteenth century had evolved it. It dates from no earlier than the beginning of the seventeenth century.

The house was taken from the midsummer of 1871 on a joint tenancy. Rossetti was at first much more often there than Morris, who was busy at Queen Square. Rossetti drew and painted, but worked in a desultory way, unhappy in the relationship with Janey, not caring for the country, in poor health, suffering from insomnia, and already taking the chloral which in the end wrecked his health completely. The strains of this situation Morris sought to relieve by visiting Iceland. Soon after settling his wife and children at Kelmscott, he went, with Magnusson and Faulkner, for a two months' stay, during which he kept a journal that contains vivid accounts of things and places seen.

Back in England, he began the illumination of an elaborate copy of the *Rubá'iyát* of Omar Khayyám, and began to write a new poem, *Love is Enough*. It was finished by the end of the year; but, readily as Morris wrote, this poem gave him much difficulty. Intended perhaps to speak out an immediate emotional situation, it did nothing of the sort; he was still revising it in the following February. Once again the idea of producing a book with illustrations by Burne-Jones attracted him; he engraved some decorative borders for *Love is Enough*, but the scheme came to nothing. At this time, too, he began a novel of contemporary life – a story of two brothers in love with one woman – which he could not finish. Fifteen years later (in *The Pilgrims of Hope*) and only by projecting it into a much larger context, he did finally succeed in finding a voice for something of the 'stormy time' as Mackail calls these years. But for Morris, though not in the end for Rossetti, it was possible to rise above a situation which seems to have brought grief and frustration to all three. His enormous energy and powers of concentration, together with an intensification of his work for the firm, and a new interest in politics, provoked by the 'Bulgarian atrocities', mark the mid 1870s.

Not only in his married life, but in his work, Morris was subject to tensions which could not have been foreseen in the gay days of the Red House. To all his partners, the firm, though important, was only one outlet for their creative work. Rossetti, Burne-Jones, Madox Brown, were painters; Webb was an architect, with an increasing practice. But to Morris the firm had become essential. In it he had found work which satisfied his creative powers, gave scope to his versatility, expressed his sense of the central importance of art to daily life. It was now also important to him in a financial way, as it had not been when it began. The income from the copper-mines was dwindling, although the exploitation of by-products like arsenic helped to maintain it; the firm was becoming the chief source of his income. He, as the others had not, had become involved in running the business, and he saw that it was necessary to make new developments. He resumed the designing of wallpapers, and began to design cotton prints. It is significant that in the decade following his taking over the firm, he produced eleven wall-paper and twenty-two chintz designs – by far the most prolific period of work in this field; while at the same time he was to study and undertake dyeing, weaving, and tapestry. Almost all this activity followed the break with his partners. By the end of 1872, with the need for expansion playing a part in the move, the Morris family left Queen Square for Turnham Green. Morris kept two rooms in the old premises for his own use, but made over everything else to the growing work of the firm as showroom and workshops. A letter written soon after the move in February 1873 describes the new pattern of his life: 'We are quite settled in our new house, and I find it very pleasant: my own room is particularly cheerful and pretty and I can work in it with a much better heart than in the dingy room at Queen Square. . . . I am very hard at work at one thing or another; firm's work for one thing. I should very much like to make the business quite a success, and it can't be, unless I work at it myself. I must say, though I don't call myself money-greedy, a smash on that side would be a terrible nuisance; I have so many serious troubles, pleasures, hopes and fears that I have not time on my hands to be ruined and get really poor: above all things it would destroy my freedom of work, which is a dear delight to me. My translations go on apace, but I am doing nothing original.' The translations were from the Icelandic sagas, undertaken in collaboration with Magnusson, which provided him with the groundwork of some of his finest poetry – notably *Sigurd the Volsung*. In the summer he made a second visit to Iceland having visited Italy for the first time, with Burne-Jones, at Easter. A letter to his mother dated Florence April 19 speaks of visiting San Miniato, which he had 'enjoyed in spite of the barbarous so-called restoration of the church and the destruction of the walls', of the beauty of the journey between Bologna and Pistoia, and finishes 'I have just come in from seeing Santa Croce, which indeed I had stumbled on for a minute before. Inside I think it is the finest church in Florence: they were singing the Miserere there.' It is characteristic of Morris that it should be the great Gothic nave of Santa Croce that most moved him in the birthplace of the Renaissance.

His Icelandic translations went on, and he began to prepare them for publication. He made also a number of illuminated copies, in a small fine calligraphy surrounded by a good deal of delicate foliation. He was working very hard at the firm's affairs, extending his range as a designer, and struggling with regular drawing from the figure 'for my soul's sake chiefly' as he said. He began an illuminated *Horace*, on fine vellum; and another of his own *Cupid and Psyche*, to incorporate designs from the earlier project.

During the summer of 1874 Morris, in spite of his concern to develop the firm, took two long holidays. One of these to Belgium in July was a family holiday, which seems to indicate some re-orientation of the relationship between himself, his wife, and Rossetti. Rossetti had for the past two years been in serious ill-health and had had a mental breakdown; suffering from delusions, he had now ceased to use the house at Kelmscott, and lived the life of a recluse.

In the autumn of 1874 Morris began to negotiate for the winding up of the firm in its original form. Burne-Jones, Faulkner, and Webb were agreeable to this; Marshall, Madox Brown, and Rossetti were not. Six months of embittering argument followed before Morris could buy the last three out. Rossetti's practical work for the firm had ceased; Marshall, since early years, had not played any marked part; but Madox Brown had made a great many designs for stained glass. He ceased to design for the firm in its new form, and for the next decade he and Morris never met; later they became good friends again; the relationship with Rossetti was never resumed.

Morris thus, at the age of forty-one, found himself in a new situation. Behind him were fifteen years of experience as a designer and decorator and of reputation as a poet; the firm was under his complete control. He wrote to Lucy Baldwin: 'I am in the second half of my life now; which is likely to be a busy time with me, I hope till the very end: a time not lacking in content too, I fancy: I must needs call myself a happy man on the whole.'

His Icelandic translations were on the point of being published. He had also just finished, and was getting ready for publication, his verse translation of the *Aeneid* (this activity he called his 'pleasure work' as distinct from the 'bread and cheese work' of the firm). It was not only the work of the firm which he now had under full control, but his personal life; the past five or six years had been full of tension and depression; now he could say 'I do verily think I have gone over every possible misfortune that may happen to me in my own mind, and concluded that I can bear it if it should come.'

He had recently produced a number of wallpapers; now he began to think of cotton prints. The wallpapers were printed by Jeffery and Company, and continued to be so until long after Morris's death; evidently he had complete trust in their ability to satisfy him as to colour and quality. Fabric printing is a more complex affair, and he approached it with very careful preparation. He had already some idea of the chief problem – colour. Embroidery had always been an important part of the firm's production; Morris had done much embroidery himself and had taught others to do so. The dye-stuffs which had come into use since the early part of the century were unreliable; the choice of colours was between those which were safe but dull, and bright ones which faded quickly and unevenly.

Morris turned to dyeing – as he did to other crafts – because only by knowing the process could he ensure control of the product. As an interim measure, he worked with a limited range of the most reliable colours to be had commercially. He set up vats at Queen Square; read every book on dyeing he could find – chiefly old books, for vegetable dyes had virtually ceased to be used – and began to experiment. The firm's manager, since the death of Warington Taylor in 1870, was George Wardle, member of the dyeing firm of Wardles, whose works were at Leek in Staffordshire. After his first experiments at Queen Square, Morris went to Leek, and there was able to work on a larger scale during 1875 and 1876. At the same time, he began to make carpets, employing a Glasgow carpet knotter to teach her craft to a number of girls taken on for this work; the carpets were made from yarn dyed at Leek. In 1876 Morris set himself to learn the craft of silk-weaving – not only the rudiments of weaving, but above all how to translate his designs by the method of 'pointing', i.e. setting out, on squared paper, thread by thread, every crossing of warp and weft. Whether for production within the firm's own shops or for production by the trade, this process was necessary – as he had learned when his first design for Kidderminster (mechanically woven) carpet came back an outrageous caricature, because he had not realised how important it was to make this mechanical transcription.

Although at this point Morris began to increase the number of crafts in which he himself could work, and one important outcome of his practice was a tremendous stimulus to what presently began to be called the Arts and Crafts Movement, it was essential for the expansion of the business that a greater variety of goods should be produced for general sale, and this meant manufacture by the trade. The number of craftsmen and craftswomen employed increased. Dyeing, carpet weaving, pattern weaving in silk and wool, embroidery, tile and glass painting, painted decoration in houses and churches – all these called for expansion. Morris could not trust to the steady continuance of work for churches and great houses; his very example had stirred the trade and he had either to grow or to shrink; he could not stand still. Hence the development of work in fields which allowed of the exploitation of the general market. Hence, too, in the summer of 1877, the opening of showrooms in Oxford Street. Queen Square, sufficient for a trade based on specific commissions, was of no use for Morris's new development; the space in the house there could be better used for necessary new workshops. It is characteristic of Morris that he should accept the logic of new needs, although showrooms, like exhibitions, were not much to his taste. 'I can't say I am as much excited about it as I should be if it were a shed with half a dozen looms in it.'

During this year alongside the new work which called for his supervision and his designing he engaged, very positively, in two public activities: the founding of the Society for the Protection of Ancient Buildings, and the work of the Eastern Question Association. Both left their mark on the rest of Morris's life.

The Society for the Protection of Ancient Buildings was directly provoked by restorations being made to Tewkesbury Abbey. A sharp attack in a letter to the *Athaeneum* on what Morris regarded as wanton destruction quickly rallied many others, and within a month the new body was in being. It still continues the work launched by Morris, keeping a watchful eye on the preservation of historic buildings. The Eastern Question Association was of a different kind and had been founded late in 1876. It was aimed at encouraging Britain to resist pressure to support Turkey against Russia in the war over the oppression by the Turks of their Bulgarian subjects. In the following May, shortly after the war had begun, Morris published a manifesto on the question, addressed not to his fellow manufacturers, designers, and traders, but 'To the working men of England'. Morris had for some time been Treasurer of the Liberal Association, but the implications of this address may well have astonished those of his fellow-liberals who read it. Although the Eastern Question Association ceased to exist after the Balkan crisis had passed, the intense activity in which it involved Morris had brought him into contact with active political and trade union figures from Gladstone down, and left him with the conviction that no fundamental change could be made in society without the leadership – not merely the participation – of the working class. This was the beginning of Morris's socialism.

A silk weaver from Lyons, named Bazin, was engaged to begin work on the new silks and a Jacquard loom was set up. Meanwhile, Morris was making many experiments with dyeing; arranging schemes of decoration for more than one great house; working at embroidery; seeing to stained glass for Putney and for Marlborough College; judging students' work at South Kensington – busy, in fact, in a score of directions. His general reputation now began to bring requests for lectures on design. The first was addressed, at the end of 1877, to the Trades Guild of Learning and appeared later in a collection of such lectures as *The Lesser Arts*.

His wife and daughters spent the winter of 1877–8 in Italy. In April 1878 Morris went out to bring them home. However, the intensive work of the past two years had been too much even for his energies, and he suffered a severe attack of illness. But before going out, he had negotiated the lease of a new house. Standing on The Mall at Hammersmith, it was (and is) a tall Georgian building, with a coach-house alongside and large garden. The coach-house was filled with looms for making carpets, and here began the making of the Hammersmith rugs. In Morris's own room a tapestry loom was set up, at which he worked for some hours every day before beginning other work. Weaving obsessed him at this period; there were so many aspects of it to be mastered, and he found it one of the most satisfying media of expression. In this pursuit he derived great stimulus from the South Kensington Museum, where he not only played his part as an assessor of student work, but was often consulted about the buying of historic examples of textiles, books, manuscripts, and carpets. The effect of this concentration showed in his designs, which even when for wallpapers or embroidery now tended to follow the demands of the loom. Where at first he had inclined to draw more or less directly on nature, he began to adopt highly stylised forms derived from mediaeval textiles.

By 1880 Queen Square and the weaving-shed at Hammersmith could no longer house all the new work. After searching up the Thames near Kelmscott, in Hertfordshire, and in Surrey, he finally settled on Merton Abbey, seven miles out of London, where the wooden worksheds of an old silk mill still stood, and where the water of the River Wandle was suitable for dyeing. His potter friend, William de Morgan, associated with him in house decoration, was also seeking a new site for his pottery and he found it near by. As a result of this, the Morris painted tiles, which had at first been quite important among the minor products of the firm, now ceased to be produced (when tiles were wanted Morgan supplied them). The works could not be transferred until dye-vats had been sunk, buildings repaired and altered. But at last everything was ready and all the manufactures except those put out to the trade were brought together on the one site. One of the first things Morris did was to plant poplar trees round the works; quick growing, they soon gave the place the garden air for which it became famous; flowers were planted, too, and a client might well go away with a sheaf of them. Working hours were less, wages higher than the norm, and a partial system of profit sharing was instituted. When, later, Morris wrote his lecture on *A Factory as it Might Be*, he knew from experience something of what could be done to civilise a place of work and, given such work as was done at Merton, to make it also a place of pleasure and of education.

The ten years between Morris's assuming complete control of the firm and his major involvement in the socialist movement of the 1880s were the busiest and most prolific of his life as a designer. Mackail credits him in this period with over six hundred designs for wallpapers, chintzes, woollen and mixed fabrics, silk damasks, velvets, carpets, tapestries, and rugs – as well as pattern work for stained glass and embroideries.

The firm's work in stained glass suffered a set-back after Morris had announced that they would no longer produce glass for historic buildings; a piece of consistency, following upon the founding of the Society for the Protection of Ancient Buildings. It led many people to believe that they had ceased to produce stained glass and for two or three years this affected their commissions.

At the beginning of 1883 Morris joined the Democratic Federation, in which he began to work hard: writing articles, speaking in the open air, and giving lectures about which he said, in response to one request, 'I have only one subject to lecture on; the relation of Art to Labour'. Differences within the Democratic Federation (it had become the Social Democratic Federation shortly after Morris joined it) resulted in a split; Morris and others founded the Socialist League, in whose journal *Commonweal* his dramatic poem of modern life *The Pilgrims of Hope* appeared. His political activities dominated the 1880s; apart from his lectures and writings for *Commonweal*, he wrote little original prose or verse; only the translation of the *Odyssey* occupied him between 1883 and 1887. His designing also slackened. Often two or three days a week – and much money – was spent on his political work: he sold most of his collection of ancient books to provide funds for this. In September 1885 occurred the scene in the Thames Police Court, where, charged with assaulting a policeman, he defined himself as 'An artist and literary man, pretty well known, I think, throughout Europe'; and in 1887 the 'Bloody Sunday' incident of Trafalgar Square in which police, backed by troops, broke up the largest demonstration (for free speech) seen since the turbulent days of Chartism. In 1890 the Socialist League became largely Anarchist, as a result of which Morris, with his closest associates, withdrew to form the Hammersmith Socialist Society, which held regular meetings, lectures, and even occasional dramatic performances, in the old coach-house, whose looms had long been removed to Merton. The whole political movement of which Morris had been, and still was, so much a part, went through a period of contraction, and he no longer spent so much time travelling, lecturing, or addressing public meetings. This did not mean a change of conviction; far from it. Replying to an American questioner on the subject in the last year of his life (1896) he wrote 'I have *not* changed my mind on Socialism' and proceeded to outline, very concisely, his beliefs which, of course, included his belief in the fundamental importance to human life of the arts.

In part this re-orientation of activity arose from the changes in the socialist movement; in part from a necessary resumption of designing and other work for the firm and from his launching into yet another field – printing – but not least from the breakdown in his health. But even at the height of his political and public activity, he had still engaged in the setting up of the Art Workers' Guild in 1884, of the Arts and Crafts Exhibition Society in 1886, and in work on behalf of these new bodies, living tokens of the effect his own work had had in the past twenty-five years. Of the second body, Morris was at first suspicious. Like most who belonged to or had grown up in the light of the Pre-Raphaelite tradition, he was never much interested in exhibitions. But, once the new societies were in being, he gave them the support they had a right to expect.

In the late 1880s he had begun to write romances of a new kind. To some extent they revert in feeling to the prose romances of his Oxford days; are more leisurely and less intense in the telling, and fall into two categories – those which have a socialist content and those which are more simply romances. *A Dream of John Ball* and *A King's Lesson*, both of which were first published in serial form in *Commonweal*, appeared as a book in 1888. *News From Nowhere*, his most often printed and widely read book, his Utopia, also appeared first as a serial in *Commonweal*; the last contribution of Morris to the paper; it was published as a book in 1891.

But in 1888 appeared the first of the pure romances – *The House of the Wolfings*, which marked the beginning of his turn towards printing. It was followed by *The Roots of the Mountains* and half a dozen similar tales.

Although two or three of these were socialist in content – in *News From Nowhere* we look forward, by the device of the waking dream, into a Socialist England; in *A Dream of John Ball* we look backward, by the same device, to the Peasants' Revolt of 1381 – the rest were written chiefly for the sheer love of telling a story. All his life Morris had done this; from childhood days when he had amused his younger sisters and brothers and from schooldays at Marlborough; now he spun romances at leisure for his own delight and that of those who could share it. Written in an archaic language from which as far as possible any word of Latin derivation has been ejected, they are a verbal equivalent of the leisurely ornament he was then designing for his Kelmscott Press.

His progress towards this had been long and devious. While still working for Street he had begun to practise calligraphy: there had been the scheme for the illustrated *Earthly Paradise*; the later scheme for *Love is Enough*; the collecting of mediaeval manuscripts and early printed books; only now, in the last five or six years of his life, was all this gathered up in the setting up of his press.

The publication of *The House of the Wolfings* set him taking an active part in the production of his books: to Jacobi of the Chiswick Press he went with *The House of the Wolfings*; applying to it the lessons learned from long study of MSS and *incunabula*. He got from him a book that pleased him greatly; but one in which he saw still room for improvement. Repeating the process with *The Roots of the Mountains*, he resolved that nothing would do in future but to be his own printer. With the help of Emery Walker, he set about the study of types; designed his Golden face, based on a type of Nicolas Jenson; got paper made to his own specification; bought an Albion press; engaged pressman and compositor, and, in a cottage on Hammersmith Mall, began printing. The first book from the press was *The Story of the Glittering Plain*, which appeared in 1891, after a year of patient and exhaustive preparation. From then, books large and small came from the press with remarkable frequency; whether plain and simple as *The Floure and the Leafe*, or elaborate as *The Golden Legend*, all were printed with scrupulous care and perfect craft. Some of them were works of his own, like *News From Nowhere*; some selections from the works of favourite poets – or even complete works; some were translations from mediaeval French or Latin. But the great work was the *Works of Geoffrey Chaucer*. The production of this, the most magnificent book printed at the Kelmscott Press, took over five years; years during which Morris's health was declining fast. Doctors had diagnosed diabetes; and though he continued to work, to design, to lecture, to write, to supervise the production of such large works as the *Adoration Tapestry* for Exeter College Chapel or the *San Graal* series for the great house of the D'Arcys at Stanmore, he grew less energetic, and by 1895 his health was quite broken. The press was his main preoccupation and in spite of illness he produced for it more than six hundred designs for initials, borders, and ornaments. The first copies of the *Chaucer* were delivered to him in June 1896, during a spell of illness; he received them in bed. A little later, on the advice of his doctor, he made a forlorn sea-voyage to Norway, accompanied by an engineer member of the Hammersmith Socialist Society, John Carruthers. The trip did nothing for his health; but he was able to see the Cathedral of Trondhjem; the last of his cathedrals. Friends brought him curious manuscripts and old books for his pleasure; Arnold Dolmetsch, musician and craftsman, played to him sixteenth-century English music on the virginals. He still had plans for a volume of mediaeval English lyrics; for a great edition of Froissart, even more splendid than the *Chaucer*; but by the summer's end it was clear that none of this could be realised. On October 3 he died.

He was buried at Kelmscott, carried to his grave on a farmcart decked with branches and flowers. Philip Webb designed the very simple slab which bears no more inscription than his name.

---

3 Precursors

Morris went up to Oxford in 1853: we need to go back a century to seek the first origins of his ideas. Ruskin proclaimed the beauty of nature and the glories of Gothic, and Morris and his friends were happy to sit at his feet. Ruskin himself had been forestalled by Pugin; and Carlyle had already in 1843 used the Middle Ages as a glass through which to take a hard look at the ethics of the new age in *Past and Present*. Also, in so far as the Middle Ages could be used, to take a similar look at the art of a society whose great pride was in its factory system. Pugin had already done this in his *Contrasts* of 1836. Ruskin united elements of both critiques: Carlyle's moral eloquence without his Philistinism; Pugin's zeal for art, without his Catholicism; and this combination gave him a special power over the English mind throughout the second half of the century.

But even before Pugin and Carlyle there had been others, and Morris's thought does not all come from one source. Not all critics of art and design were, like Ruskin, Pugin, and Carlyle, anti-industrial; some were men deeply interested in the development of science and manufacture. Their concern was of an optimistic, not a pessimistic kind.

It is not hard to find the sources of both patterns of criticism. It was the eighteenth century which produced the factory system, the still-evolving magic of machinery and steam power, and shifted half the country's population into towns of a kind never seen before. The same period saw the beginning of the Gothic Revival which was at its height in Morris's youth. The ultimate importance of the Gothic Revival lies neither in its formal exercises nor in the success with which the best of its practitioners made living design out of a dead style, but in its conversion of a sentimental, romantic, nostalgic historicism into a firm basis of criticism not just of the arts, but of contemporary society.

The efforts of some of the more energetic and responsible industrialists of the eighteenth century had already directed attention to a new need; the exercise of taste in the products of industry; and ever since its inception in 1753 the Society of Arts had played a part in catering for this need. To improve design had from the Society's beginning been as important as to improve materials or techniques. Concern of this kind led to the Royal Commission which investigated the training of artists and designers in 1836, and to the setting up of the Government School of Design in 1837.

The new tendencies to theorise about design rather than art, and to speak of art manufactures (a term which came to be much used in the 1840s) arose from the impact of new methods of production. As yet, the idea of the decline of craft skills had not emerged. The basis of concern had, on the whole, been positive: that the machine was the newest evidence of progress, an enormous boon to man, was taken for granted. In spite of reaction against this complacency, the compelling occasion of concern was that, by the 1830s, those countries Britain had outstripped in terms of production and cheapness began to challenge this industrial supremacy, equipping themselves with machinery and setting up their own factory system. And it began to be thought that though we might maintain our lead in this respect, we could not compete with continental countries over design and ornament. Hence the Commission; hence the School of Design – presently to multiply.

At no time has the Royal Society of Arts played so important a part in this field as in the middle of the last century. When we spell out its full title – The Society for the Encouragement of Arts, Manufactures, and Commerce – the nature of that part becomes clear. The Society had from the first offered prizes for and held exhibitions of inventions and discoveries in chemistry, mechanics, agriculture, and every kind of craft and trade, as well as drawings and designs. Looked at in the light of the development of machine production, its ideas about design may seem misconceived; the concern was almost entirely with ornament and decoration, not with structure and function. But it was a real concern, and by the 1840s was expressed in moves to make greater use of exhibitions as a stimulus to individuals and to industry as a whole. A series of semi-permanent exhibitions of manufactured goods had been held in London between 1828 and 1833; up and down the country, literary and philosophical societies, local academies, had arranged exhibitions among whose miscellaneous contents were specimens of industrial products as well as of traditional crafts, works of art, and curios. Finally in May 1845 the Society resolved to promote a periodical exhibition of works of industry, offering prizes for 'art manufactures'.

A competitor for one of these prizes was Henry Cole, a Keeper in the Record Office who, under the pseudonym of Felix Summerly, entered a tea-service of his own design, made by Minton. He won a silver medal for this, and his success inspired him with the idea of setting up an association of artists, designers, and manufacturers to produce domestic goods of high quality.

In 1847 the Society held an exhibition of 'Select Specimens of British Manufactures and Decorative Art', in which an important feature was that as well as articles entered by individuals for the Society's awards, there were factory goods submitted by manufacturers. The two hundred and fourteen exhibits included pottery, glass, cutlery, silversmithing, furniture, and wallpapers. Twenty thousand people saw this exhibition; it was repeated over three years. The next step was to win Government support for such an exhibition on the largest possible scale. Henry Cole and the architect Matthew Digby Wyatt, newly returned from a similar exhibition in Paris, were ambitious for the British to outshine the French. Important manufacturers were canvassed for support and promises of entries. Prince Albert gave the scheme his blessing, and in his capacity of President of the Society submitted to the Home Secretary a request for a Royal Commission to promote the exhibition. This was granted in January 1850, and there followed over a year of intensive preparation; the building of the fabulous and novel hall which came to be called the Crystal Palace was followed week by week in *The Illustrated London News*; as exhibits arrived they were photographed, drawn, engraved, reproduced; cheap railway excursion tickets meant that working people from all over the kingdom could visit the exhibition; and it was opened May 1, 1851. It was an enormous success, and to its promoters, a glorious demonstration of the power of modern society.

In considering Morris and his work, the Great Exhibition as a whole is of less importance than the fact that it included a good deal of work for leading manufacturers by men who were not trade designers working to rule of thumb or following fashion; but were by training and profession painters, sculptors and, even more frequently, architects. The manufacturers had become design-conscious, and used these 'outsiders' not simply to add ornament to their trade wares, but to design the actual objects, concerning themselves with form as well as with surface. Notable examples are: Alfred Stevens designing stoves and grates for Hoole and Company of Sheffield; Pugin designing furniture, silverware, fabrics; Owen Jones designing wallhangings and papers for Crace, the leading furnisher. All this was not yet industrial design, as we think of it; it was 'art manufacture'. But art manufactures were a step on the way.

Augustus Pugin, a refugee from the French Revolution, had been an accomplished draughts-man and designer. For many years he worked for John Nash, architect to the Prince Regent, providing him with Gothic designs and details with which Nash himself had no sympathy. After leaving Nash, Pugin published some elaborate, well-engraved books – *Specimens of Gothic Architecture* (1821) and *Specimens of the Architectural Antiquities of Normandy* (1828). His son Augustus Welby Northmore Pugin was born in 1812; grew up with such skill in drawing that some of the plates in his father's Norman volume were made from the boy's drawings, and he became extremely well versed in the ornament of Gothic architecture. As early as 1827 he began to design for the goldsmiths, Rundell and Bridge, and at the same time designed furniture for Windsor Castle, then being restored. Romantic and impetuous, he engaged in a variety of work, including a period as a scenic designer at Covent Garden, where his sets for the opera *Kenilworth* were a tremendous success. Later he set up in business, selling Gothic carvings (of his own design) and was imprisoned for debt; he married the daughter of Dayes the scene painter with whom he had worked, was within months made a widower, but married a second time in 1833, and built himself a house of Gothic design near Salisbury.

In the following year he became a convert to Roman Catholicism. There seems no doubt that his passion for Gothic and mediaeval art and architecture influenced him – as aesthetic preferences influenced a great many people, including Morris and Burne-Jones in their youth, in the same direction. But for Pugin the art and beauty of the mediaeval world were inseparable from the unity of the Christian Church, the sense of a common social order, a common ethic. His love of Gothic was not just antiquarian, but moral; as the world of railways and factories and industrial towns grew around him, he turned from it in horror and disgust to what he at least believed to have been a better social and moral state; a society which had produced beautiful buildings, sculpture, painting, and furnishings because it was better, purer, more whole than the society of nineteenth-century England. Pugin published a number of books between 1835 and his death in 1852. He designed a number of churches, chiefly for the Roman Catholic community, and a great deal of jewellery, plate, furniture, fabrics, and wallpapers; built himself a second Gothic house at Ramsgate, and a private church dedicated to St Augustine. When in 1834 the old Houses of Parliament were burned down, and Barry got the commission for the new buildings, he came to him for help with the detailing, and Pugin designed not only all the architectural details and carving, but tiles, light-fittings, furniture, during the next two years. At the time he published his books of designs for plate and furniture – *Ornaments of the Fifteenth and Sixteenth Centuries* – followed in 1836 by one of his most significant books, *Contrasts*. The book of designs might be looked on simply as patterns intended to cater for a more solidly formed Gothic taste than hitherto; but *Contrasts* was not primarily concerned with taste. Not only is Gothic architecture contrasted with other styles, but as mediaeval *Catholic* architecture it is shown to be the architecture of a better state of society. This was followed by his *True Principles of Gothic Architecture* and his *Apology for the Revival of Christian Architecture in England*; with eloquent language, beautiful drawings, and fine designs he preached his twofold gospel, making himself felt everywhere as the most brilliant exponent of Gothic.

In 1851 he was commissioned to arrange the Mediaeval Court at the Great Exhibition – one of the most splendid parts of the Exhibition; but in the following year he became insane and died, at the age of forty, having accomplished an enormous amount of work, not least significantly in the designing of metalwares, furniture, stained glass, and textiles. Much of this was done for industry; but he had also a workshop where he could keep direct control over standards of production.

Both as theorist and as practical designer, Pugin is one of the two or three most important precursors of Morris.

Owen Jones was a precursor of a different sort. He, like Pugin, was extremely influential as a propagandist of design; but, unlike Pugin, he was not identified with the Gothic Revival. Like Pugin, he was an architect, though not, like Pugin, a particularly successful one. It was as designer and writer on design that he made so strong a mark on the mid-century. He was born in London in 1809, studied at the Royal Academy Schools, worked under Lewis Vulliamy and then, in 1833, travelled to the Middle East, visiting Greece, European Turkey, and Egypt; the next year he spent largely in Spain. His close acquaintance with the Arab and Moorish architecture of the Mediterranean directed his attention to the field of ornament, and gave that interest its marked bias towards abstract and geometric forms. In 1842–5 he published his *Plans and Details of the Alhambra*; in 1846, *Polychromatic Ornament of Italy*; in 1856, with the help of a number of other archaeologists, architects, and designers, appeared his *Grammar of Ornament*, which became the best known and most constantly used of the many manuals and folios of drawings and designs with which an architect or decorator would equip himself. In it, ranging from Polynesian carved wood to Italian arabesques and Egyptian palm and lotus, in splendidly lithographed plates, he reviewed the characteristic ornament of every part of the world. In this book too he set out his principles 'in the arrangement of form and colour, in architecture and the decorative arts', in thirty-seven propositions. Some of these propositions are no more than rules by which the designer may produce a given effect; but others are of a larger kind, such as: Proposition 1: 'The decorative arts should arise from, and should be properly attendant upon, Architecture'; or Proposition 3 – which repeats traditional academic doctrine: 'As Architecture, so all works of the Decorative Arts should possess fitness, proportion, harmony, the result of all which is repose'; – or Proposition 5: 'Construction should be decorated. Decoration should never be purposely constructed'. Proposition 37 perhaps may be said to fall into a category of its own. It is that 'No improvement can take place in the Art of the present generation until all classes, Artists, Manufacturers, and the Public, are better educated in Art, and the existence of general principles is more fully recognised.'

Like Pugin, Owen Jones had an important post in the organisation of the Great Exhibition; he was Superintendent of the Works, with supervision of the decoration of the building; he was also Superintendent of Class Thirty of the exhibits – which included Sculpture and Plastic Art, Mosaics, and Enamels. When the Crystal Palace was dismantled and re-erected at Sydenham, it was Jones who designed the interiors of the Greek, Roman, Egyptian, and Alhambra Courts.

He designed a good deal – furniture, wallpaper, textiles, books, and complete interiors. It was as a pattern designer that he excelled, and all his work shows a strong bias towards flat colour and geometric forms. Even when designing in the Gothic manner, he is severe and formal, always hardening the forms of nature with well-defined conventions – in accord with his Proposition 13: 'Flowers or other natural objects should not be used as ornaments, but conventional representations founded upon them.' He was in fact the leader of the modern school of designers, who were concerned to analyse natural forms and draw out their innate geometry as the basic element of pattern.

But there were immediate associates of Morris, members of the Pre-Raphaelite circle, who should be remembered among the precursors in design, though we know them as painters. They were all members, as were Morris and Burne-Jones, of the Hogarth Club, which existed from 1858 to 1860. The Pre-Raphaelite Brotherhood had been formed ten years earlier to assault the entrenched academics and revive English art. To whom, more than to Hogarth, should such rebels look for historic support? That there is nothing in Hogarth of the Gothic taste of the 1840s is not important; the Gothic element was not so strong in this group as is usually thought; on the contrary, they were rather suspicious of it; it carried, especially for Hunt, the taint of Rome. The Ruskinian notion of truth to nature was much more central for them; and it is in this connection that Hogarth's importance to them can be made clear. Ambivalent as his attitudes are in some respects, a somewhat similar concept lies at the heart of his *Analysis of Beauty*. He had been primarily concerned with experience. Art, for him, must derive from the impact on eye and mind of the living world. The doctrine of the *Analysis* is not so much aimed *against* contemporary taste as *towards* the establishment of experience, unmediated by the academic conventions, as the basis of art.

Stylistically, the only one of these painters who ever showed any hint of likeness to Hogarth was Ford Madox Brown; he was important to them not as an example of style, but as an exponent of an anti-academic outlook. So it was his name that they took for their club in 1858.

A little while before the club was wound up, Ford Madox Brown had resigned. He had sent in some designs for furniture, which had not been hung, since they were not regarded as art. Art was painting and etching; not designs for chairs.

Yet many others of the club had been interested in design, and regarded it as well within the artist's scope. Rossetti and Holman Hunt also made designs, and had already, in discussions, anticipated the kind of creative partnership which did eventually emerge with the building of the Red House.

Holman Hunt, as a boy of fourteen, had come into direct and unexpected contact with the practice of pattern design when working in the London office of Richard Cobden. In his autobiography, *Pre-Raphaelitism and the Pre-Raphaelite Brotherhood*, he tells of a day when into the office where he worked came a stranger from Lancashire, who proceeded to sit down with colours and brushes and set about making designs for cotton prints. Young Hunt was excited by this novelty, and for weeks after practised designing. Later, a serious student at the Royal Academy Schools, he still interested himself in design. 'My past experience in pattern designing,' he wrote, 'and my criticisms upon the base and vulgar forms and incoherent forms in contemporary furniture, to which I drew Rossetti's attention on his first visit to me, encouraged visions of reform in these particulars, and we speculated on improvement in all household objects, furniture, fabrics, and other interior decorations. . . . We agreed that architecture also came within the proper scope of a painter. . . . In our scheme, when we obtained recognition, each of us was to have a set of studios attached to his house, some for working in ourselves, in diverse branches of art, some for showing our productions to admirers, who would be attended by our pupils when we were too busy to be disturbed. We were also by such means to introduce worthy students, and to make art take its due place in life.' There was a particular reason why Hunt should be thinking about these things; his family lived above an upholsterer's showroom. 'The articles and the furniture and hangings there displayed could not but challenge observation as wanting in artistic taste to a degree greater than could be found in any previous age or country whatever. With my practical experience in designing patterns for fabrics, I had grown to regard all decorative design as part of a true artist's ambition, and I declared that until our craft again employed itself in devising beautiful forms, taste in furniture, in costume, and even in architecture, would remain as bad as, or grow worse than it had been for the last fifty years, during which time the practice of design had been left to tradesmen only.'

Ford Madox Brown left records of his interest, more precise and perhaps more reliable, since they are to be found in his diaries, and describe the designing of actual pieces of furniture – only a few of which have been reliably traced. In March 1857, for instance, he notes having worked on the *Transfiguration* design for Powells – his first stained glass – and a new table; nine months later he records four new designs for chairs. Some of these pieces were made for Holman Hunt and other friends, and when the firm was set up he continued to make designs for furniture as well as for stained glass. It was partly from Brown's designs that the early furniture of the firm took its very simple character; basic construction, strength, and convenience were his guiding principles; there was nothing about his work of the large-scale grandeur to be seen in many of the architect-designed pieces of the period. He thought rather in terms of designing cheap good furniture for working men. Unfortunately, this very fact makes it less likely that his furniture should survive in any great quantity, we know it from a few drawings and one or two samples only.

In design, then, whether one thinks of pattern design and decoration, or of furniture and furnishings in general, Morris and the Morris firm had behind them a number of exemplars; the uniqueness of the firm's work consisted in the way it was done, not in the fact that it was done.

---

4 Stained glass

As far as Morris's own designs are concerned, he excelled in wallpapers, chintzes, woven fabrics, and embroideries, but it was for a long time the firm's stained glass which compelled notice. In the 1860s this was the most important part of their production. Without it the firm might well have been unable to develop the very substantial place which it made for itself in the market in the early 1860s. Their connections with some of the most progressive architects made it natural for them to work in this field on the basis of actual commissions, alongside the bigger specialist stained-glass producers such as Clayton and Bell, and Heaton, Butler and Bayne. It was their stained glass and embroidered hangings which most impressed the judges in the 1862 Exhibition; and as early as 1864 the South Kensington Museum – not yet the Victoria and Albert – bought four panels of stained glass. These are: a very bold and simple head of *Penelope* in a roundel against a ground of quarries in which daisy-clump and thistle alternate; and three tall panels of *Chaucer Asleep*, *Dido and Cleopatra*, and *Alcestis and Eros*.

It was in the late 1860s that Warington Taylor managed the firm – after the opening of the Queen Square workshops. In his anxiety to put the business on a sound footing, he wrote anxious letters chiding the partners for their failure to organise. Many of these were to Webb, whom he seems to have thought more business-like than the rest, and from these letters we get a good deal of information about these early days; glass is a frequent subject. Of 1866 Taylor writes to Webb:

'Over £2,000 work in glass done. This should have returned at least 25 % therefore over £500 profit. You know well enough there was not £200 profit on glass.' He then sets out a number of practical questions which he says must be asked – and answered – to ensure that the stained glass shall bring the firm not only reputation but the kind of profit which it should – and which they badly need. How is the work measured? What are the charges made? Are the designs charged separately from the actual production? How much extra – and therefore chargeable – work is entailed by more elaborate drawing or patterns?

At the end of 1867 the actual value of the glass rose to about £2,300, though the number of windows produced in the year remained around twenty from then on. In Taylor's view, this amount of work ought to have brought the firm more profit, especially as it was by far the most important part of their production. He recommended charging a rate of £2 10s to £3 per foot, the designs to be paid for separately. Apart from their failure to cost jobs and to organise the flow of work, what seems to have most irritated Warington Taylor was the failure of the partners to make adequate charges to clients and above all to ask enough, individually, as fees for designs. Until he succeeded Faulkner – who had gone back to Oxford to take up a Fellowship – design fees were paid out of the firm's price to clients. In 1862, Rossetti and Burne-Jones were each paid five pounds for a single light; Morris, who subsidised the firm as he had subsidised *The Oxford and Cambridge Magazine* and was later to subsidise the Socialist League, took two pounds less. This compared very poorly with the fee which Madox Brown, early in 1857, had charged Powells of Whitefriars for his *Transfiguration* design – sixteen guineas.

Until Taylor, no thought seems to have been given to the rate of profit to be taken by the firm on each window, or the fact that the designer was designing for the client, not for his friends and partners. Taylor was concerned that proper fees should be paid for designs, and proper prices charged to clients, and that an exact account should be kept of all expenditure. He was further exasperated by delays in producing designs, in the completion of work undertaken, in making proper use of their workers. Although Morris himself was responsible for production, he tended in his enthusiasm to start more jobs than could be finished at one time, while his nervousness about meeting delivery dates meant that he would often suddenly take a man off one job and put him on another – to the detriment of the work and the efficient use of his own valuable time as a designer. Taylor, who had the devotion of an over-loving mother to this band of artists, was infuriated by all this, but he succeeded to a large extent in getting the work to flow smoothly, and Morris to work in a concentrated way. The lessons he gave them were well learned by the time he died – and learned with gratitude. What in the first five years Morris had tried to achieve by sheer hard work, Taylor showed could be better done by organisation and foresight.

In 1866 the firm received two extremely valuable commissions – for the decoration of the Armoury and Tapestry Room at St James's Palace, and for the Green Dining Room at South Kensington. The latter, in addition to much painted and modelled ornament, contains stained glass to Burne-Jones's designs. These are characteristic of his early work, before he was influenced by Botticelli, but much freer than his first stained glass from the influence of either Rossetti or Madox Brown. Like the windows designed in 1862 for Birket Foster's house at Witley, and those made for the Red House, these windows belong to a category of glass which was to become quite important for them; though the greater part of the glass was ecclesiastical, the firm produced a good deal for secular and domestic settings. While the St James's commission was in itself the most valuable, the Green Dining Room, as it came into use, could not help but be an effective and continuing advertisement for the firm; so too their decoration of their own showrooms in Queen Square. They began to be asked for complete decorative schemes for big houses in both town and country, and Webb's developing practice as an architect brought in further work in decoration and furnishing.

Stained glass, one of the first products of the firm, was among the work specially prepared for the 1862 Exhibition, which was important to them not only because of the awards which the glass and other goods won, but because it began to change the character of the association. The decision to exhibit meant a challenge to the trade on the practical plane; it meant also that in future work should come to them not simply through commissions, but from the public – a change which led to a crisis in the early 1870s, which at this stage they could not foresee. But to exhibit, work must be made, and in some quantity. The hands of the partners and their first few workmen were not enough to undertake what they now had to do. By the end of 1861, four new craftsmen had been taken on; this was a factor in compelling them to seek a larger volume of work, putting them on a more commercial footing.

The foreman, George Campfield, was a glass painter originally with Heaton, Butler and Bayne and encountered by Burne-Jones at the Workingmen's College; among the newcomers was a glazier named Holloway, who also became a glass painter; and Morris and Charles Faulkner both took part in the painting of glass as well as of the tiles which were decorated at Red Lion Square. With the experience of four of the partners in designing for stained glass, and their close association with Powells, they were in a good position to develop this side of the work. They did so with such effect that the trade was alarmed. It is clear from Lewis F. Day's monograph (*Easter Art Annual* for 1899) that the furnishing and decorating trade was suspicious of Morris, Marshall, Faulkner and Company from the outset. In 1866, soon after he began work as a youth with Lavers and Barraud, a firm of stained-glass makers, he heard of the firm as 'a set of amateurs who are going to teach us our trade'.

The award of the medals in 1862 brought a very unpleasant reaction. The glass in particular had been commended for 'its artistic qualities of colour and design'; and their work in general, described as 'in the style of the Middle Ages', had been praised for its archaeological exactness. The stained glass came under attack from the trade for the same reasons that had drawn this commendation from the judges. A petition was raised against it, on the ground that it was in fact genuine old glass touched up and remounted. However, the petition came to nothing, and in repudiating it one of the judges, Clayton, of Clayton and Bell, described it as the finest of its kind in the exhibition.

At the same time, they received an order from G. F. Bodley for designs for windows in his first church, St Michael and All Angels, Brighton, which was nearing completion; while the design by Rossetti, illustrating the *Parable of the Wicked Husbandmen* which had formed part of the firm's exhibit, was used in his second church, St Martin's, Scarborough – where Morris also decorated the pulpit with painted panels. A third church by Bodley, All Saints, Selsley, Gloucestershire, brought another commission in 1862. In addition to the seven-light east window for which Rossetti's design was used, two other windows in St Martin's Scarborough were also filled with stained glass by the firm; the designs, by Ford Madox Brown, being of an original and unmediaeval character, at least in the drawing of the figures. In each light in a rectangular panel of less than half the total area, the naked figure stands, robust and un-ascetic, with thick flowing hair, Eve clasping a white dove in her arms, and Adam, whose face is that of the artist himself, rolling over with his foot a small bear. The rest of the window is occupied by uniform quarries with a boldly painted motif, a two-leaved spray which terminates in a crown.

At this period, with five of the artists contributing designs, the firm's glass had a great deal of variety, which tended to be lost as Rossetti did less and, after 1875, Madox Brown ceased to contribute at all. The type of window just described was frequently produced. It belongs in essentials to the old Gothic tradition, and is described by Charles Winston in his book on *Ancient Glass*. It was a type of which Winston approved, since it gave a good deal of scope for what he describes as the mosaic style and less encouragement to the designer to see his window as a painted picture. The single figure lent itself to working in large, well-defined areas of colour which also displayed its form, the drawing being identified with the leading; whereas the quarries might bear a simple leaf or flower or abstract motif, thus allowing the window still to admit generous light while projecting colour into the building. The designs for quarries which the firm made at this period were similar to those for painted tiles, another important product, for which Webb, Morris, Burne-Jones, Rossetti, and Brown all provided designs. They link directly too with the now-lost wallhangings of the Red House, whose dark blue or red serge was embroidered with scattered knots of flowers in bright colours; and with the first of the wallpapers, the *Daisy*.

The use of repeating patterns is very marked in Morris glass, in response to mediaeval precedents and Winston's guidance: combined with bold areas of pure, bright colour, in glass of carefully controlled quality, this helped to establish its distinct character. Both before and after the advent of the firm, good and bad glass was produced which had the abstract pattern of the Owen Jones school, or, at the other extreme, was no more than elaborate painting, so overworked as to muddy the colour and darken the whole window in a senseless endeavour to treat it exactly as if it were an oil painting. The first kind appealed to the more Puritanical and Evangelical clergy, as containing no idolatrous imagery; to many of the most modern designers, as making full use of the pure, abstract virtues of the colours of the glass. The second, which continued to be produced throughout the century, was often designed by artists otherwise admirable, and there was a good deal of this kind to be seen in the 1862 Exhibition; it appealed particularly to people who could not share or had already begun to react against the Gothic taste, but who carried a conception of painting as naturalistic illusion-making into other media. Even in good examples of this sort of window, the failure to respect the elements of the medium itself undermines images which, simply as pictures, might otherwise have been admirable.

Even when the firm's glass became more pictorial, the principles laid down by Winston were always observed. Shading and stippling were minimised. Pattern, on the other hand, even when the background of regular quarries was not used, played a very big part. In flowing or powdered patterns on the robes of saint and angel, or in the foliage and flowers of backgrounds, boldly drawn, lively motifs keep the eye continually entertained, as in the fine windows at Middleton Cheney in Northamptonshire. In the figure of St Agnes, the diagonal meander of a leafy twig which ornaments her robe is contrasted with the more geometric pattern in the lining of her turned-back sleeve. There is nothing finicky about this subsidiary work; it provides contrast with the major forms of the figure but never becomes trivial. Behind the saints in these windows, another favourite device, repeatedly used by Rossetti, Morris, and Burne-Jones in this period of close association, adds more enrichment without obscuring the splendid simplicity of the figures. Behind the figures, which stand in pairs, runs a containing hedge or screen of tall saplings, thickly leaved and bearing fruit. Here the hedge is of pomegranates, and leaf and fruit make a pattern which anticipates the character of the tapestries of the next decade. On the narrow strip of ground at the feet of the saints, daisy and violet radiate their tight clusters of leaves and throw up their flowers – as in the verdures of fifteenth-century tapestries.

This free elaboration of pattern provided Morris with scope for his special talent; but his work in stained glass was not only the provision of patterns. He designed a fair number of figures (including several of the Middleton Cheney figures), controlled the all-over colour, set the leading, and drew the designs together for the actual making. He chose the glass, supervised the painting, passed the window before firing, and it is to him that the magnificence of colour, and the beautiful interplay between large masses and minor patterns is due. This interplay, of which he was such a master, is one of the marks which distinguishes his work from that of other good Victorian designers.

Twenty years after this first bold entry into the field of design, Morris and Company took space in the big Boston Foreign Fair of 1883. The work shown included a number of windows, and drawings and cartoons for glass, chosen to show the variety of scale and treatment. On these, as on all the exhibits, there is a commentary which is not a detailed account of the windows, but a short essay on the principles of stained glass.

'As regards the method of painting and the design, our glass differs so much from other kinds that we may be allowed a word of apology. Glass painting differs from oil and fresco, mostly in the translucency of the material and the strength, amounting to absolute blackness, of the outlines. This blackness of outline is due to the use of lead frames or settings, which are absolutely necessary for the support of the pieces of glass if various colours are used. It is therefore a condition and characteristic of glass painting. Absolute blackness of outline and translucency of colour are then the differentia between glass painting and panel or wall painting. They lead to treatment, quite peculiar in its principles of light and shade and composition. In the first place, the drawing and composition have to be much more simple, and yet more carefully studied, than in paintings which have all the assistance of shadows and reflected lights to disguise faults and assist the grouping. In the next place, the light and shade must be so managed that the strong outlines shall not appear crude, nor the work within it thin; this implies a certain conventionalism of treatment, and makes the details of a figure so much more an affair of drawing than of painting; because by drawing – that is, by filling the outlines with other lines of proportionate strength – the force of the predominant lines is less unnatural. These, then, are the first conditions of good glass painting as we perceive them – well-balanced and shapely figures, pure and simple drawing, and a minimum of light and shade. There is another reason for this last. Shading is a dulling of the glass; it is therefore inconsistent with the use of a material which was chosen for its brightness. After these we ask for beautiful colour. There may be more of it, or less; but it is only rational and becoming that the light we stain should not be changed to dirt or ugliness. Colour, pure and sweet, is the least you should ask for in a painted window.'

One does Morris more justice by tracing such ideas to their source than by pretending that they arose in his mind by some process of inspiration. His principles of designing and making glass are those he had learned as a young architect, and had first practised and seen put into practice in the late 1850s, when he had helped Burne-Jones with his first commissions for Powells of Whitefriars.

In the great revival of stained glass, a critical part was played by Charles Winston, barrister of the Inner Temple, amateur archaeologist, friend of such architects as Philip Hardwick and Benjamin Woodward – who was also Rossetti's friend.

Winston spent many years in the study of ancient stained glass. His interest in distinguishing between the styles of the different periods of Gothic led him to research into the actual substance of glass. He submitted these researches to Powells of Whitefriars, who had at that moment special reasons for interesting themselves in them. The Whitefriars Works, under Excise regulations in force from 1745 to 1845, was classified as a flintglass works, and could not legally make window glass, blown or rolled. In 1844, in order to get round this rule, the company began to produce quarries for church glass by stamping them out in iron moulds; and Winston was consulted as to their aesthetic suitability. From this point, Powells were able to take part in the growing trade in stained glass for church windows. Winston's researches had begun in 1838, and in 1847 resulted in his authoritative book on *Ancient Glass*. Winston followed Rickman in his stylistic account of the periods of Gothic architecture, relating the development of stained glass directly to it, and this historical account takes up two-thirds of his space. The remaining part, however, is directed to the designer, describing techniques and principles. The principles, as was natural at that time, were ecclesiastical as well as technical. Winston sets out orthodox Anglican ideas on the use of art in churches, rejecting symbols as unsuitable for Protestant churches, and adds the oblique argument that even if one did not feel very strongly on this question, it would be best to exclude Roman Catholic symbols from one's designs in order to minimise prejudice against the revival of the art!

Winston goes on to discuss what he calls the mosaic system of glass painting. By this he means a technique of building up the design substantially by areas of pure colour which identify themselves with meaningful parts of the drawing, can be defined by the leading, and so make the maximum of effect with the minimum of shading or stippling. The use of the term glass painting, which Winston keeps in preference to stained glass, implies anything but the painting *on* glass against which he repeatedly warns the designer. It is painting *with* the glass that he intends; if it were possible he would exclude all additional drawing and brushwork.

Obvious as these ideas may appear to us now, especially as in the last two decades we have become used to windows which are composed in exactly this way and entirely without drawing in the painterly sense, there was every reason then for the emphasis. Winston's was not the first account of glass; but it was the first analysis of it as a medium. The craft had degenerated after the Reformation into mere imitation of oil painting, dulling the colour, denying the essential character of the medium. The eighteenth century had sunk to the lowest depths in this. Morris and his friends were familiar with an example which Winston cites – the west window of New College Chapel, Oxford, designed by Reynolds. All in all, it was well that Winston should say:

'The artist who undertakes to practise glass painting should bear in mind that he is dealing with a material, essentially different from any with which he has hitherto been familiar; and his first object should be to obtain a thorough knowledge of the peculiarities and of the extent of the available means of his art; of the excellencies which ought to be developed, and the defects which should be concealed.'

This was the conception of stained glass which Rossetti, Madox Brown, Burne-Jones, and Morris took to heart; and in their work they observed Winston's principles implicitly. In so doing, of course, they were following a concept which is reiterated by other writers of the period on art and design – Pugin, Ruskin, and Owen Jones – that of using the true nature of one's material, avoiding the imitation in one medium of effects proper to another.

Winston's book provided such serious architects as Morris's master Street with information and guidance in an art with which they had more and more to deal; Webb and Morris had probably already encountered it in Street's office before they met Rossetti or became directly involved in designing stained glass. It was through Rossetti that, some years before the setting up of the firm, several members had begun to work in the medium. Rossetti's rooms and studio on the riverside at Blackfriars were close to the Temple and to Whitefriars Works. Powells, as they sought to develop the stained-glass side of their trade – freed of restriction in 1845 – needed artists who could design for them. Woodward was asked to suggest names, and he put forward that of Rossetti, who in turn recommended Ford Madox Brown and Burne-Jones, then very much his pupil. Burne-Jones's first designs were for the dining-hall of Bradfield College, and were made 1856–7; Madox Brown's first design was the single-light *Transfiguration* already referred to. The cartoons for these windows would be set out for leading by Powells; but when the firm began to design for their own production (after which Burne-Jones at least did no more designs for anybody else), it was Morris who undertook this, turning them into what Winston had called mosaic glass, and selecting from Powells' stock the actual glass to be used – glass produced, until his death in 1864, under Winston's guidance. It was not only the mediaevalism of the designs that provoked the charge of using fragments of real old glass; it was the quality of this glass itself, made with great care to Winston's specifications.

Rossetti, Burne-Jones, Madox Brown (whose chief preoccupation was easel painting) might have been seduced from Winston's severe principles. Morris and Webb, trained as architects and thinking as designers, were not. There is no doubt that the excellence of Morris windows lies in the use of strong masses of pure colour, the frank use of the leading as integral with the drawing, the use of the medium in its own terms and not as an imitation of something quite different.

Others who designed windows for the firm were Webb, who shared Morris's task of turning drawings into finished cartoons and of supplying pattern elements, Arthur Hughes, Simeon Solomon, and Peter Paul Marshall (though very little of his work is known and he only produced designs for the first two years of the firm's existence).

In designing and producing stained glass, as in other work, the firm was not unique but took part in a very considerable movement; other Victorian designers also produced glass of quality. However, in the early days of this development, it was the firm's glass which most clearly struck out a new line, achieving its effects not by elaboration or the pursuit of pictorial magnificence, but by treating the medium in terms of its own potential.

As the Arts and Crafts Movement developed in the 1880s and 1890s, many other painters and designers worked in stained glass, and often, in proportion as they too followed Winston's 'true principles', with equal success; though the total volume of the firm's production is greater than that of artists working in a more individual way. Pursuing the logic of Morris's notion that the responsible designer should know the medium through practice, members of the Century Guild, Art Workers' Guild, and other similar societies of the last quarter of the century undertook work in stained glass, many as specialists. Not all that was produced was good or interesting; much of the later production of the minor members of the Arts and Crafts Movement was dull and barren when it pretended to the simplicity which had been so vital a feature of the earliest of the Morris glass; and as the powerful impetus of nineteenth-century religious movements faded, the stained-glass tradition in England sank into pastiche of stained glass instead of imitation oil painting, its earlier vice. There is little to choose between the two.

But in the late 1940s and early 1950s there began a new movement, stimulated by the urgent need to rebuild war-damaged churches and cathedrals, and by the positive interest of a number of the clergy and of diocesan architects in the use of the arts in a modern way. A good deal of stained glass of the last twenty years has, in a twentieth-century context, been liberated entirely from the pictorial tradition. Winston's principles as to the use of glass in its own right have been carried to a point which, in terms of taste and style, would doubtless mystify him and his whole generation, could they but see it; nevertheless, the stained glass of the 1950s and 1960s, using new techniques of fusion, making play with the thickness and refractive power of the substance as well as its capacity for bearing colour and transmitting coloured light, is truly a logical conclusion to the process set in train by Winston's investigations into ancient glass; his analysis not merely of the glass as substance, but, far more important, of its real potential as a design medium. The successful application of his principles, by Morris and his friends, has led us to the windows of Evie Hone, Margaret Traherne, John Piper, and Patrick Reyntiens. Glass whose thickness plays with the light, whose irregularities and facets break it up; windows in which the glass is allowed full scope, in which the artist takes advantage of all the qualities which distinguish it as a material and a medium from the stone or concrete in which it is set, on the one hand, and from the painting which it no longer imitates, on the other – these are as much a part of the Morris legacy as the galaxy of twentieth-century typefaces or the functional product design which looks so different from what came out of Queen Square or Merton.

---

5 Pattern design

Morris was a master in the art of enriching a surface. Work of this kind occupied him from the earliest days of the firm to the time of his death, although much of his energy was spent in directing the firm's production, in craft experiments, in the sheer manual work of dyeing, weaving, and in designing – very often in collaboration with Philip Webb – complete schemes of decoration.

We must discount, for we know nothing of them, his earliest designs, the work he did during the two and a half years of tormenting endeavour to become a painter, or anything he may have done while in Street's office. Still in existence now is the one painting *La Belle Iseult*, in the Tate Gallery; a few drawings, and the pieces of furniture made for the rooms in Red Lion Square which were transferred to the Red House, there to initiate the programme of design and decoration out of which the firm grew. We know that he helped Burne-Jones with the drawings for some of his earliest stained glass; but we do not know which parts of these designs Morris himself may have done.

His work as a designer dates from the move to the Red House. After the setting up of the firm, he seems to have given up three-dimensional design. From then on his activities seem to have been divided between the development of actual production and the making of pattern designs. Much later, in Merton Abbey days, he designed for his own comfort a squat semicircular chair in which he sat while weaving – it is now in the William Morris Gallery, a unique and rather amusing example of functional design in three dimensions.

It seems probable that Morris's rudely functional view of the nature of furniture limited his interest in this field – this, and a proper respect for Webb's gifts. For him, a chair must be stout enough to sit in firmly – and withstand his startling habit of straining its joints, literally, to breaking – while being light enough to move about the room if need were. He had no liking for the specialisation of rooms to which modern life has committed us. All rooms were, for Morris, rooms for living, and it should be possible to use the same one for eating, relaxation, and conversation, work, study, or sleep – witness the erection in his bedroom of a tapestry loom, and the fact that he habitually drafted patterns and corrected proofs in the same room as family and friends. Furniture, then, although it must be strong, was stuff to move around. Its forms were dictated by human proportion, by the need to sit, to lay out food for a meal, books for reading or papers and colours for designing and by the need to keep some things safely in a cupboard or a cabinet. But as to form and proportion, the fundamentals of design, these he seems to have seen no need at all to meddle with.

The simple forms of chest, cabinet, cupboard, or hooded settle, offered large flat areas or well-defined panels which to him and his friends were invitations to decorate. The *St George Cabinet* made for the Red House, the *Seddon Cabinet* with its pictures of the Honeymoon of King René, offer typical examples of such enrichment. This was not particularly an invention of Morris, or of the members of the Pre-Raphaelite Brotherhood before him, but was already the practice of other artists and designers. The architects led the way; it was they, more than the painters, or the trade designers, who created the new trend and were responsible for the new Gothic furniture, wallpapers, and fabrics. The example had been set by Pugin, Owen Jones, Butterfield, and Burges. Where the painters still tended to look at design as the applying of art to given objects, the architects were more inclined to take a fundamental look. The new furniture of Morris and his friends was simpler than that which preceded it; in part the simplicity was governed by basic construction; in part it was a way of providing flat surfaces for Rossetti, Burne-Jones, or Madox Brown to paint.

The painting of these pieces was mainly pictorial, but it was also thought of as flat decoration. The scrupulous imitation of nature that was so important a part of the early Pre-Raphaelite gospel was not suitable for this; nor did any of them attempt such naturalism in their furniture painting. Rossetti's own discovery of the work of Blake must have helped a good deal in the evolution of a type of painting which worked very well when applied to panels. Rossetti's pictures of the late 1850s and 1860s – packed, non-illusionistic, rich in colour, the main figures fitting tightly into the available space, the areas between them filled with detail, so that the whole surface was close-knit with enrichments – had influenced both Madox Brown and Burne-Jones; they covered the panels of cabinets and the doors of cupboards with painting of this kind. The same simple, intense convention also characterises almost all the firm's early glass, especially in the small panels.

Furniture and glass called for subsidiary pattern and ornament; so too did much else of the growing work of the firm. Morris, an expert not only in designing but in actual embroidery, produced the designs. Painted panels, painted beams, plaster work, many early commissions for altar cloths and hangings, and tiles, all called for invention, but not of a pictorial kind. Morris was at his least happy in drawing the human figure (although there are more figures in the firm's glass from his hand than was once thought). He would leave this side of the work to Brown or Burne-Jones, and he came, naturally, to take over the pattern design. This he often shared with Webb, who with no pretentions as painter or figure draughtsman was expert in small animal and bird forms.

Painted patterns for woodwork, embroideries, quarries for glass, and painted tiles, all exercised Morris's special skill before he ever started designing wallpapers or fabrics. Glass was important to the firm from the beginning; the fact that by the end of the 1860s all the friends were engaged in stained-glass design must have helped in moving them to their common enterprise, and when the workshops were set up in Red Lion Square, a kiln was installed for firing quarries and tiles. It has been suggested that painting tiles was an inappropriate technique; but quite apart from any scruples Morris had about the use of transferred patterns for ceramics, it should be remembered that orders for tiles varied, were not on any large scale, were often individual in kind, and painted designs answered the purpose much better than printed ones. No special equipment was needed; Morris, Rossetti, Faulkner – could all handle a brush, and painting gave a livelier quality than would have been achieved by mechanical copying. Often the tiles, as in Birket Foster's house at Witley, were a mixture of picture and pattern.

These early tiles were simple, light in character, freely drawn in blue or grey, and when they bore pattern motifs instead of forming part of a picture, they were very closely related to the glass quarries. One such design was Morris's *Daisy*; it was one of the simplest, freshest, and most lasting of his designs; formal but vigorously and naturally rendered daisy-clumps of two kinds alternate in regular rows.

This *Daisy* pattern was used again in the first designed, although not first produced, of Morris's wallpapers. The paper is more complex than the tiles, though still innocent in its pattern structure. The forms of flower and leaf have been elaborated; there are more colours and the background is relieved by a coarse stipple, in accordance with Morris's idea that the poverty of the paper as a material must be so relieved, though in a woven fabric the true texture of the thread structure needs no such help.

The *Daisy*, the *Trellis*, and the *Fruit*, Morris's first wallpapers, date from 1864. They herald seventy patterns for wallpapers, chintzes, and woven cloths made in the following thirty years, and were made just before the firm moved to London from the Red House. All three designs have a strong *naïve* character, though in each it is displayed in a different way. The *Trellis* has hints of Morris's work in embroidery; the other two show the influence of his work in tiles. This is most obvious in the *Daisy*, whose powdered structure relieves him of the need to link and mask his repeats. The motifs remain as forms seen against a background; he had not yet learned how to make all elements of the coloured surface play an equal part in the design. In the *Trellis* we have a continuous motif provided by the trailing rose stem; the naturalistic birds; and the wooden trellis, which gives the name, performs two necessary acts at once: extending its uniform grid over the whole area, its rectangular form also provides a strong contrast with the meander of the plant and the naturalistic forms of leaf, flower, and bird.

The *naïveté* of Morris's first attempts is most marked in the *Fruit* or *Pomegranate*. Each repeat is divided into four equal parts, in each of which a diagonal stem throws off leaf and fruit so as to present a fairly even distribution of forms – similar motifs are used in the Green Dining Room at South Kensington. Essentially this is a tile pattern, based not on the usual upright rectangle, but on a square. The quartering of the repeat so as to use four fruit forms instead of one has the effect of making the pattern look at first as though the repeat were one-quarter its real size; only as the eye dwells on it do we see that each of these four quarters offers a variant on the theme of the leafy, fruited twig. *Naïve* as this is, in some ways, the apparent *naïveté* lessens as we consider a larger area. The quartering then has the effect of disguising the true repeat while asserting its geometric structure. In the first draft of this design, the fruit in one quarter was an olive; but before the pattern went into production, it was changed so that all four parts had the same visual weight. At this stage, Morris's experience of pattern designing was limited: but he had the instinct which moved him towards a viable solution, even although his formal ordering of natural elements is unsophisticated and innocent.

By 1872 the other members of the partnership were playing very much less part in the running of the firm than Morris. By this time it was no longer a simple, rather carelessly run artists' co-operative, but a well-established and influential business. Two or three years later, the dissolution of the original partnership and the change of name to Morris and Company only marked formally a reality which had been consolidated over the preceding decade.

The resumption of wallpaper design and production was a part of the process by which the firm developed yet further the character which had been signalised by the move to Queen Square. All the production of early days had been on the basis of firm orders or commissions; but the 1862 Exhibition committed the firm to a different policy: that of establishing a range of goods which could be kept in stock and be readily repeated to meet the general demand. Stained glass, large embroidered hangings, painted cabinets, time-consuming and expensive to produce, did not meet this requirement. Glass quarries, tiles, small embroideries, table glass, jewellery, light chairs based on the Sussex pattern, could be produced in quantity, repeated, did not lock up much capital or engage skilled workers for long periods. Morris, doubtless urged to think in these terms by Warington Taylor – who had been responsible for the adoption of the Sussex chair – and becoming more and more concerned for the success of the firm as a business sought now to expand the range of goods produced and at the same time to maintain high quality.

The production of woven and printed textiles and wallpapers was an important part of this development. Tapestries and embroideries were prestigious and lucrative; but once the firm had come to employ a certain number of workers skilled in particular techniques, the pattern of production must use all to the best advantage. And Morris, far from being a dreamer who happened to make a success of design by accident, was a very practical, decisive person; letters to his mother on family business, letters to Thomas Wardle of Leek about costs, production, and saleability of designs show him as very clear-headed and business-like.

Part of the impetus towards the production of fabrics arose out of his wish to control the quality of colour in the silks and wools used for the firm's embroidery, always an important part of the business. His experiments in dyeing date from 1874. He went into it with typical thoroughness and energy, reading all he could on the subject in seventeenth- and eighteenth-century manuals; culling information from older herbals, finding useful information in Gerard, Fuchsius, Pliny, and Herodotus. A scullery at Queen Square was fitted up for experiments, and he began to try out the old recipes on silks and wool. He had also begun to plan chintzes – the first design being the *Tulip and Willow*, made in 1873 and printed by Thomas Clarkson of Preston; but Morris had been dissatisfied with the result and did not market the print until he was able, at Merton, to produce it himself. In the meantime, new designs were printed by Thomas Wardle of Leek.

Wardle was the brother of Morris's assistant, George Wardle, now manager; and had a reputation as a dyer. In order to make experiments on the scale he needed if he were to do his own dyeing, Morris went up to Leek several times during the next two years, studying techniques and working in the vats himself. Goods already sold by the firm had proved unsatisfactory because of fading. This, and the garish or muddy character of available chemical dyes, determined Morris to control the process himself. 'I am most deeply impressed with the importance of our having all our dyes the soundest and best that can be, and am prepared to give up all that part of my business which depends on textiles if I fail in getting them so.' As it was only during the preceding two or three years that he had turned to textiles, and this as an essential of trading policy, it was a very serious matter.

Morris made a careful choice of those commercial dyes which were reliable, and allowed them to dictate his colour schemes, using them in whatever combinations he could. At Leek and Nottingham he learned the use of the virtually obsolete indigo and madder vats; and even when at Kelmscott he would still experiment with old vegetable recipes. 'I was at Kelmscott the other day,' he says, 'and betwixt the fishing, I cut a handful of poplar twigs and boiled them, and dyed a lock of wool a very good yellow.'

When he was able, in 1876, to set up a dye house, although on a small scale, at Queen Square, he did all the dyeing himself. Later, having taught this craft, as he taught so many, to assistants, he turned to other things; but for two or three years dyeing occupied a great deal of his attention. It was coupled with the setting up of looms for carpet knotting, and weaving in wool and silk. All the weaving done was pattern weaving. There would have been no point at all in the hand-weaving of plain fabrics, in which competition with the machine would have been impossible. The alternative, the setting up of power looms, was for a different sort of reason impracticable. It would have required a great deal of capital, far beyond what he had at his disposal, and would have resulted in the domination of the whole enterprise by totally irrelevant considerations; it would in fact have destroyed the firm.

Had Morris been simply a craftsman, concerned solely with individual designing and making, the firm could never have grown, nor would he have been at all likely to undertake the very activities by which we now know him best and in which without doubt he rises to the greatest heights. He would have confined himself to embroideries, tapestries, windows, illumination, and individual schemes of decoration. He would certainly not, as he did from early days at Queen Square, have added to the goods for sale the Indian and Italian pottery and other small domestic and decorative wares which he stocked. Though his goods were out of range of the working class, it would be a great mistake to imagine that he was not concerned to sell to the general public the best he could. His most elaborate embroideries, such as those made by Mrs Holiday, or the large hand-knotted Hammersmith carpets, which he boldly claimed as the best carpets except the old Persians, were certainly made for well-to-do and wealthy customers; but it was of the essence of the enterprise, as he saw it must develop, that it should rest at least as much upon ordinary trading.

Nearly ten years passed between Morris's first three wallpapers and his other pattern designs; and those first designs are different from all others. They show very directly their relation to activities going on in the decoration of the Red House, and bear little relation to the characteristics of wallpapers already on the market. Their *naïveté*, their naturalism, is marked in contrast to the formal austerity of the most fashionable designs. Pugin, Owen Jones, and Dresser were anti-naturalistic in their work; Pugin's love of Gothic, Owen Jones's love of Moorish design, both moved taste in the 1850s towards the abstract and the geometric. Owen Jones's *Grammar of Ornament* contained a number of plates illustrative of natural forms as the material of the designer; some of these were contributed by Christopher Dresser, trained at the National School of Design, and a considerable botanist. In his own book, *The Art of Decorative Design*, Dresser was at pains to exercise the same principles of analysis as Owen Jones, carrying them very much further, not seeking the harmonic rule of the classicist, but an alternative order of geometric arrangement. To him the art of design consisted in abstracting such a geometry from the growth of plants, regularising the arrangements discovered and disposing them over a surface. This was the sort of idea which affected the trend of design when Morris first began to practise.

When he resumed pattern designing in the early 1870s, Morris's designs were affected by his interest in the design of textiles and carpets, as well as by his increasing use of the new South Kensington Museum. But it would, I think, be a mistake to attribute this change of style simply to an obsession with woven forms. It seems to be no less due to Morris's serious study of the kind of goods which the firm ought to produce. Committed to a policy of designing outside commissions, Morris was confronted with the problem of how to satisfy the market without succumbing to its worst aspects. He had the choice of following or leading; being Morris, having his superb gift as a designer, he chose to lead and did lead, making designs neither merely naturalistic, nor coldly formal. Only in one or two designs does Morris produce work as cold, flat, and abstract as those of Pugin and Owen Jones; in no case, not even in those first innocent three, does the love of natural form destroy the formal order.

Morris not only practised as a designer; he delivered a number of lectures, composed with much care, in which his ideas were set out. The lectures were printed, some published as pamphlets, others issued in book form. In 1881, when he had been in practice as a designer for twenty years and had a considerable reputation, he lectured at the Workingmen's College, on *Pattern Designing*. As in all his lectures and writings, he is concerned to discuss craft in terms of its historic development, design in terms of its meaning in everyday life and its contribution to human happiness. There is no such thing as a lecture or essay by Morris which concerns itself solely with technique or solely with history.

'You may be sure,' he says in *Some Hints on Pattern Designing*, 'that any decoration is futile, and has fallen into at least the first stage of degradation, when it does not remind you of something beyond itself.' This might be taken as an attack on the abstract element in pattern making; but he does not intend that mere naturalism shall be sufficient.

'Now, to sum up, what we want to clothe our walls with is 1) something that it is possible for us to get; 2) something that is beautiful; 3) something which will not drive us either into unrest or into callousness; 4) something which reminds us of life beyond itself, and which has the impress of human imagination strong on it; and 5) something which can be done by a great many people without too much difficulty and with pleasure.

'Now I have been speaking of what may be called the moral qualities of the art we are thinking of; let us try, therefore, to shorten their names, and have one last word on them before we deal with the material or technical part.

'Ornamental pattern work, to be raised above the contempt of reasonable men, must possess three qualities: beauty, imagination, and order.

''Tis clear I need not waste many words on the first of these. You will be drawing water with a sieve with a vengeance if you cannot manage to make ornamental work beautiful.

'As for the second quality, imagination: the necessity for that may not be so clear to you, considering the humble nature of our art; yet you will probably admit, when you come to think of it, that every work of man which has beauty in it must have some meaning also; that the presence of any beauty in a piece of handicraft implies that the mind of the man who made it was more or less excited at the time, was lifted somewhat above the commonplace; that he had something to communicate to his fellows which they did not know or feel before, and which they would never have known or felt if he had not been there to force them to it. . . .

'Now as to the third of the essential qualities of our art: order. I have to say of it, that without it neither the beauty nor the imagination could be made visible; it is the bond of their life, and as good as creates them, if they are to be of any use to people in general. Let us see, therefore, with what instruments it works, how it brings together the material and spiritual sides of the craft.

'I have already said something of the way in which it deals with the materials which nature gives it, and how, as it were, it both builds a wall against vagueness and opens a door therein for imagination to come in by. Now, this is done by means of treatment which is called, as one may say technically, the conventionalising of nature. That is to say, order invents beautiful and natural forms, which, appealing to a reasonable and imaginative person, will remind him not only of the part of nature which, to his mind at least, they represent, but also of much that lies beyond that part. I have already hinted at some reasons for this treatment of natural objects. You can't bring a whole countryside, or a whole field, into your room, nor even a whole bush; and, moreover, only a very specially skilled craftsman can make any approach to what might pass with us in moments of excitement for an imitation of such-like things. These are the limitations which are common to every form of the lesser arts; but besides these, every material in which household goods are fashioned imposes certain limitations within which the craftsman must work. Here again, is a wall of order against vagueness, and a door for the imagination. For you must understand from the first that these limitations are as far as possible from being hindrances to beauty in the several crafts. On the contrary, they are incitements and helps to its attainment; those who find them irksome are not born craftsmen, and the periods of art that try to get rid of them are declining periods.

'Now, this must be clear to you, if you come to think of it. Give an artist a piece of paper, and say to him "I want a design," and he must ask you, "What for? What's to be done with it?" But if you say, I want this queer space filled with ornament, I want you to make such and such a pretty thing out of these intractable materials, straightway his invention will be quickened, and he will set to work with a will; for, indeed, delight in skill lies at the root of all art.'

Having made these basic points, of the need for order, of the necessary stimulus of the limitations of material and function, Morris then goes on to analyse the simple grids upon which flat patterns can be built up, relating these to historic examples from Italy, Sicily, Byzantium, and ancient Egypt. He then goes on to speak of what he calls 'the relief of patterns, which may be considered as the other side of their mechanism. We have, you see, been talking about the skeletons of them, and those skeletons must be clothed with flesh, that is, their members must have tangible superficial area; and by the word relief I understand the method of bringing this out.'

If, then, when he first began as a designer, Morris showed a warmer feeling for natural forms than was fashionable, it did not mean that he failed to understand that construction also played a part in what he regarded as the imaginative life of the pattern. From the very beginning he shows an instinct for appropriate form, making his pattern cover the whole field, not compelling the eye to dwell on each unit, but persuading us to wander from repeat to repeat without insisting too forcibly on the formal grid. Later, when much experience had brought him a fuller intellectual understanding of the processes of pattern making, he recognised that the masking of the repeat might rob us of some of the visual stimulus we should get from a pattern. What at first he did intuitively, he later came to modify; there are designs in which the repeat is allowed to assert itself strongly; and it is in those patterns most affected by his study of historic woven patterns – both those in which the repeats are symmetrically disposed and those which make use of the meander or ribbon. But in few patterns does he allow such harsh definition of form as was used by his older contemporaries; there are no Morris designs in the Moresque or Alhambra style so much cultivated by Owen Jones and his followers; none which are simply abstract. All take their start, as to form, from some piece of living nature; in general, a flower, a plant, some derivative of whose natural growth enables the designer's hand to move over the geometric grid with as much freedom as discipline; with the freedom which comes of discipline. Constant reference to nature was vital: among other things, it was the only real protection against mere imitation of historic forms.

Morris was helped by his own observation of nature and by the old herbals; in collecting these, he had not only accumulated knowledge of the properties of plants for dyeing, but added to his repertoire of conventions for dealing with natural forms. The older conventions of drawing, requiring a clear display of the plant's forms and the bold wood-cut technique by which they were reproduced, must have helped towards that easy mastery which allowed him as no other designer could, to give a very close representation of plant and flower without weakening his pattern. Morris loved plants. Mackail, in his life of Morris, quotes a series of passages from letters, any one of which might be a programme for chintz or wallpaper. For instance:

'The fields are all butter-cuppy. The elms are mostly green up to their tops: the hawthorn not out, but the crabs beautiful, and also that white-beam (I think they call it) with the umbelliferous flowers. In the garden we have lots of tulips out looking beautiful; the white bluebells and some blue ones; some of the anemones are in blossom and they all soon will be: they are very lovely. Appleblossom for the most part only in bud, but that cherry tree near the arbour opposite my window is a mass of bloom. The heartseases are beautiful; a few of the Iceland poppies are out: the raspberries are showing for blossom.'

And other passages one might easily find in his writings have the same quality; vividly and with delight in the physical reality, he puts before us a pattern of words that provokes an excitement identical with that which we receive from the printed and woven fabrics, the papers and the tapestries.

Entirely at one with his contemporaries in his recognition of the part played by geometric order, Morris required a design to play on the imagination; for him, therefore, there must always be some image. Although for him repose is an essential quality which the designer should pursue, this does not mean that designs should be blank and static; rather that they should give us something of the relaxed pleasure of a garden. A wallpaper should be able to turn a room into a bower, a refuge, without insisting on its presence in the room with us. A chintz should not hang flat, but should be allowed some play, so that the actual fabric asserts itself through the design, which should be read in flowing but discontinuous passages. Morris thinks not only of the pattern, but of its *use*. It is in his awareness of the inbuilt suggestions and rhythms necessary to a living design, that Morris is different from and better than his fellow-designers.

Morris's designs were not produced freely in the sense of being unrelated to factors of material, function, and technique. These factors, some deriving from the technique and some from the needs of the trade, were a part of the stimulus to create. When setting out a design, on paper, he must of course do it exactly, steering his forms over the whole surface, linking repeat and repeat, accounting for all. But the pattern is not to work only on the surface, even in the case of wallpaper. In the case of chintz or silk or woollen hangings, this is catered for by the natural undulations of the fall of the material, and by its real texture: the eye is not, and cannot be, always at one focus. But wallpaper offers no such natural relief; it must cling flat to the wall surface.

Morris caters in the simplest and subtlest ways to give the eye relief. Intuition, long practice, and sharp perception and his determined analysis of the mechanisms of design, showed him that there is a principle. Wallpapers, he says in his lecture on *Pattern Designing*, must operate within a little depth. There must be a slight illusion – not as to the forms of the motif, but as to relative depth. And quite consistently we find in his patterns that one element is developed and spread like a net over another, with differences of scale and weight as to parts, so that we are always aware of a major pattern playing over a minor one. It is important to any designer to have a repertoire of forms on which he can draw; his problem is to keep them alive through endless repetition and variation; and it is here that Morris is so much the master. One or two basic grids for construction; a large flowing line to be developed as broad scrolling leaves or as a proliferating stem; contrasting leaf and flower forms, large and small; perhaps a robust small bird; a secondary net of leaf or flower forms to offset the main theme – this was Morris's bag of tricks. But however constantly used, they were as constantly renewed by reference to nature and the study of historic ornament.

Deeply learned as he was in the history of design, Morris never, like so many of his contemporaries, worked imitatively. He was no more sympathetic to art-as-archaeology than to art-as-abstraction, and both these trends were kept in check by his delight in living nature and constant use of familiar plants. For about ten years after the production of woven patterns became the dominant part of his work – the period, roughly, between the firm's becoming Morris and Company, and the move to Merton – his designs showed greater formality; the need to meet a variety of more or less mechanical requirements played as much part in this as his deeper study of historic textiles. Then the patterns became relaxed once more; but however close to nature, they never fell into mere naturalism. His last pattern design the *Compton* wallpaper designed for Laurence Hodson in 1896, combines all that his own theories demand; it is a masterpiece comparable with the great anonymous masterpieces of the Middle Ages.

Right from early days in Queen Square, Morris designed for machine as well as for hand production, and a great deal of material was produced for the firm by trade printers and weavers. After the first unsuccessful attempt to print wallpapers from etched plates, this work was all handed over to Metford Warner of Jeffery and Company, who printed all the Morris papers until 1930. Six designs Morris had printed by machine; but all else were hand-printed in order to maintain colour control and printing quality. Once the Merton workshops were set up chintzes, printed velvets, and linens were largely produced there. But, from early days, work was put out to the trade – except for what Morris printed himself at Merton, all the chintzes were printed by Wardle. In weaving, Morris designed much that could not have been produced in sufficient quantity at Merton – let alone in the limited space of Queen Square – and therefore much was put out; muslins, for instance, were never woven by Morris himself. Carpets, too, were largely woven by the trade. Morris designed for many different kinds of carpet – Wilton, Kidderminster, Axminster, and Patent Axminster, as well as the Hammersmith knotted carpets and rugs. He learned how to take advantage of the technical limitations of each kind and in early Queen Square days, even linoleum, a new cheap material which offered no obvious scope at all in terms of craft, was tried.

and for the Hammersmith carpets, came into a
lifference in Morris's basic thinking about design;
oblems of a somewhat different order, for where
were made for particular shapes rather than being
)n. It also meant that there were differences in
Morris as a designer and as a craftsman running

nmediate and intimate control in the making, and
. the part of the craftsman, whose function Morris
He liked to take advantage of this. Boys with no
at Merton not only learned the skills of weaving,
,wer and plant, to translate the given design with
.asters of their craft than if they had simply repro-
the design. Morris detested nothing more than the
1d Gobelins works of a medium which, with mosaic,
ts. Not only would he not countenance the use of
1sel picture, but, as also in the firm's stained glass,
orker in choice of such elements as flower motifs in

et the best results; but there was another side to the
nust put something of himself into his work, and as
newal of that self. This was to Morris of the deepest
)roduction to take this into account was a large part
and the social system within which it was used. He
detestea .. .. . . the man to the status of a part of the machine; nor
did he delude himself that . ppened when actual power-driven mechanisms were
employed; handicraft, mechanically used, could do as much to reduce the human status of the
craftsman – turning him into a mere 'hand'. No craftsman at Merton was ever allowed to
become that.

The following extracts from the Morris and Company brochure for the Boston Foreign Fair,
1883 are particularly interesting as an insight into how Morris himself thought the products
should be used.

THE HEAVY CURTAIN STUFFS sometimes called Tapestries, though that is a misuse
of the word, are hung on the outside of the booth, where the full effect of their folds and
patterns can be fairly judged. These cloths are made of various kinds of wool – some fine and
closely woven, others rough, and open in texture, to suit all the purposes for which heavy or
heavyish curtains are required. The material in every case is pure wool, prepared in various
ways, to give the variety of effect which is observable. The dyeing is all done by ancient or
well-tried processes, and no expense has been spared to get from the East the dyestuffs most

suitable for each color. Some of the bold designs of these hangings are not strangers to America, the *Peacock*, more especially, having already won for itself a place; but others, like the *Violet* and *Columbine*, are quite new, and have not been shown anywhere before the opening of this exhibition. One use of these heavy cloths in England, is the hanging of the walls of churches or large halls. Mr Morris's own room is hung with the *Bird* pattern, from the skirting to within two feet of the ceiling. The cloth is hooked to the top rail, and is but slightly plaited – only just enough modulation of the surface being allowed to just break the pattern here and there. The beautiful effect of a long wall hung in this way is quite inconceivable, and we much regret that we have not space for showing this use of the material.

CARPETS The carpet to the left as you enter is a real Axminster, so called to distinguish the make from the various kinds of patent goods which have been invented since the method introduced from the East was first practised at Axminster in Devonshire. Some Patent Axminsters are very good for the price, but they differ essentially from the original fabric, and the palm still remains to it for durability and beauty of material, irrespective of pattern; though if pattern be also considered, the greater freedom of working gives the handmade carpet an advantage quite beyond competition. The handmade Axminster exhibited is a soft, close pile, made in one piece. It is inferior to the Hammersmiths in weight, and in variety of pattern and color; but it is as much superior to Wiltons and Patent Axminsters in all the qualities desirable in a carpet. Wilton carpets must be classed as the best kind of machine-woven carpets. The patterns they bear are somewhat controlled as to size and color by the capability of the machine, and they are necessarily made in strips, not more than twenty-seven inches wide, as a rule. A Wilton carpet is therefore sewn together, and the border is also sewn on. If well made the material is very durable, and by skilful treatment in the designing, the restrictions as to color are not noticeable. In consequence of these restrictions a Wilton carpet is more embarrassing to a designer than are the happier products of the handloom; and good designs – that is, designs having a form and character proper to the material, and good and beautiful in themselves – are more rare in this cloth and in Brussels than in hand-woven fabrics. When Mr Morris began to design for Wilton carpeting, he aimed to produce pure and shapely forms with simple coloring, doing the best he could with the material, without straining its capacity for decoration. Among the patterns on the floor are three colorings of a bold design adapted to one of the best makes of Patent Axminster. This cloth may be easily distinguished from real Axminster by the uninitiated, if the backs of the two be compared. The Patent Axminster has a foundation of hemp; the real Axminster is all wool. As the Patent Axminster is also a coarser fabric, the designs for it are necessarily much bolder than for Wiltons and real Axminster. When a large pattern is wanted, therefore, and Hammersmith carpet cannot be had, this patent cloth should be chosen.

The remaining carpets exhibited in the first room are varieties of Kidderminster. The heavier sorts are three plies, the lighter two plies. These carpets are very solid, well-woven goods, and of great durability if properly laid. The colors are dyed in the same way as for the most expensive rugs, and the patterns are carefully adapted to the material.

THE HAMMERSMITH CARPETS are named from the place where Mr Morris first began the manufacture. They are now made at Merton Abbey in Surrey, where we have recently established our factory. On some of the smaller rugs will be seen the Hammer and M, significant of the earlier place of manufacture. The later carpets have no trade mark. The quality and style of carpet we have called Hammersmith is a speciality of Morris and Company. There are no such carpets made elsewhere, not even in the East, though the best Indian carpets may be compared with them in weight. In all other respects they have no rivals, except the few ancient carpets which may occasionally be found in the stores.

DAMASK for wallhanging, is now a revived taste in Europe. Not that the use had ever quite died out; but just before the revival, damasks were seldom used except for palaces and the richest houses, and they were always silk damasks. One of those we exhibit is a mixture of silk and wool. We call the increased use of these wallhangings a revival, because the covering of walls with stuffs, tapestries, or whatever would hang, must have preceded the use of paper for walls; paper hangings by their name being evidently a substitute for something better, but more costly. The three walls of this room are covered with damasks of different designs. It is perhaps necessary to say that this is because we wished to exhibit as many varieties as there was space for. The rooms must not therefore be taken as consistent decorations, but simply as showrooms. The large pattern in gold suffused with pink is a silk damask of the best quality – the name of the pattern, *St James's*. It was first used, though not in these shades, for the Throne room at St James's Palace. The smaller pattern on the wall to the right, a Damascening of dark bronzy green, steely blue, copper and gold tints, is also a silk of the purest make. We call the pattern *Flowergarden*. The colors suggest the beauties of inlaid metals. On the opposite wall is the silk and wool damask. This is very novel in effect, and an admirable wall covering, even where pictures are hung, though the pattern is large and full of variety, a tone of warm, broken grayness is the prevailing effect. It is quite warm enough to harmonise with the gold of picture frames, and gray enough not to hurt the color of a picture. The introduction of the fine wool through the pattern is the main cause of the subdued splendour.

WALLPAPERS, as they are nearly connected with the wallhangings we have been describing, in speaking of them something further may be said on the subject of wall decoration.

In the Decorative Arts, nothing is finally successful which does not satisfy the mind as well as the eye. A pattern may have beautiful parts and be good in certain relations; but, unless it be suitable for the purpose assigned, it will not be a decoration. Unfitness is so far a want of naturalness; and with that defect, ornamentation can never satisfy the craving which is a part of nature. What we call decoration is in many cases but a device or way we have learned for making necessary things reasonable as well as pleasant to us. The pattern becomes part of the things we make, its exponent, or mode of expressing itself to us; and by it we often form our opinions, not only of the shape, but of the strength and uses of the thing. . . .

Pattern choosing, like pattern making, is an architectural art. A pattern is but part of any scheme of decoration, and its value will be derived in great part from its surroundings. Personal liking, therefore, is not an infallible guide in the choice of wallpapers. . . . For ordinary cases the following simple rules may be laid down, which will perhaps answer most questions. If there is a reason for keeping the wall very quiet, choose a pattern that works all over without pronounced lines, such as the *Diapers, Mallows, Venetians, Poppy, Scroll, Jasmine*, etc.

If you may venture on more decided patterning, and you ought always to go for positive patterns when they may be had, choose the *Daisy, Trellis, Vine, Chrysanthemum, Lily, Honeysuckle, Larkspur, Rose, Acanthus*, or such. In deciding between those whose direction or set is horizontal, and those which have more obviously vertical or oblique lines, you must be guided entirely by the look of the room. Put very succinctly, architectural effect depends upon a nice balance of horizontal, vertical, and oblique. No rules can say how much of each; so nothing can really take the place of feeling and good judgement. If you have no professional aid, you must decide for yourself whether the room most wants stability and repose, or if it is too stiff and formal. If repose be wanted, choose the pattern, other things being considered, which has horizontal arrangement of its parts. If too great a rigidity be the fault, choose a pattern with soft easy lines, either boldly circular or oblique-wavy – say *Scroll, Vine, Pimpernel, Fruit*. If the fault lie in the too great predominance of horizontal lines, without any marked stiffness in the parts, as when the walls are very low and long, choose one of the columnar patterns, as *Larkspur, Spray*, or *Indian*; or, better still, hang the walls with chintz, or cloth, in folds. . . .

On color . . .
Contrasting color, if strong, must be kept within small quantities; if pale or gray, it may be more freely used. Chairs and sofas give great opportunities for introducing points of bright contrasting color, and for those high lights and darkest shades which are essential to a complete scheme. Covers need not be uniform. They may be of two or three kinds, according to the size of the room and the number of pieces.

If the chief color be red, it will be desirable to have large areas of white for rest to the eye. Blue, gray, green, and lighter tints of red should be the variants. Contrast with it should be generally avoided; it wants quiet rather than excitement. Whenever white paint may be used for the woodwork, choose it in preference to any other. The use of positive color is very difficult, and house-painters are peculiarly ignorant of it. Their incapacity may have led to the use of the dull, gray, even dirty shades, which have become so general since house decoration began to interest educated people. The revolt against crude, inharmonious coloring has pushed things to the other extreme, and instead of over-bright colors, we now have the dirty no-colors. The aim was to get sobriety and tenderness, but the inherent difficulty was not less great than before. It is not more easy to paint grays that shall have color, than to paint color that shall be gray; and whichever it be, *color* is still the essential. In this difficulty, the use of white paint is the only way of safety. White is perfectly neutral; it is a perfect foil to most colors, and by judicious toning may be assimilated with any.

---

6 Printing

'I began printing books,' said William Morris, in a note written in 1895 to help an American lecturer, 'with the hope of producing some which would have a definite claim to beauty, while at the same time they should be easy to read and should not dazzle the eye, or trouble the intellect of the reader by eccentricity of form in the letters. . . . As to the fifteenth-century books, I had noticed that they were always beautiful by force of the mere typography, even without the added ornament, with which many of them are so lavishly supplied. And it was the essence of my undertaking to produce books which it would be a pleasure to look upon as pieces of printing and arrangement of type.'

A little earlier in an address to the Bibliographical Society, he had set out in very simple terms his criteria of excellence in book design. '. . . a book quite unornamented can look actually and positively beautiful, and not merely un-ugly, if it be, so to say, architecturally good. . . . Now, then, let us see what this architectural arrangement claims of us. First, the pages must be clear and easy to read; which they can hardly be unless, Secondly, the type is well designed; and Thirdly, whether the margins be small or big, they must be in due proportion to the page of the letter.'

Since the last book was issued from the Kelmscott Press in March 1898 considerable changes have taken place in taste and in the design of books, and of printed material in general; there was surely never so positive an interest in print and its uses as now, nor such a lavish range of typefaces and papers available. This attention to the practice of printing, the recognition of the typographer as a designer, and a considerable literature on the subject of types, typography, printing history and techniques, is generally acknowledged as one of the most important parts of Morris's legacy. His importance in promoting good printing and in directing the attention of printer and public alike to the possibilities, advantages, and delights of well-designed and well-printed books has been recognised in Britain, in Europe, and in North America, ever since the days of his own activity. The general principles he set out would meet with approval from typographers everywhere.

But approval of principles does not always result in approval of practice, and hardly any commendation of Morris's principles, or acknowledgement of his special part in the promotion of this branch of design, has appeared without some qualification of praise when it came to the consideration of his actual work. In the 1920s and 1930s, when the typographer in common with other designers was fighting hard for the acceptance of clean 'functional' design, and type designers were very conscious of designing for machine-setting, the typical Kelmscott book appeared as nothing but a stumbling-block. Certainly, it was anything but the model for mass-production. The designer might well have been prepared to make formal acknowledgement that the private press movement in general and the Kelmscott Press in particular had done something to set ideas in motion in his field; but he could find little sympathy for the actual product. Even among the private presses, it seemed obvious that the Ashendene Press, still more the Doves Press, came closer to the new ideal of simplicity and austerity.

Now, as taste and fashion swing back, and we allow ourselves in the 1960s to luxuriate in patently unfunctional forms, producing designs which set on edge the teeth of typographical puritans, we may find it perfectly possible to look at Morris's printing with a pleasure denied to those bred in the gospel of sans serif. We should not, all the same, allow ourselves to assume from this that Morris would have been likely to get the same pleasure from all the typography of the 1960s. We may be far from sharing Morris's architectural concept of the book – fundamental to his feeling for typography – and derive much of our new look from the conscious revival of Art Nouveau – which he detested. We can only come to useful conclusions as to Morris's importance, by having regard to principle, and distinguishing between the fundamental and the simply fashionable. We must, however much we admire the books of the Kelmscott Press, distinguish between its direct products and the more various products of its influence. Some of these, whose legitimate descent is easily traceable, look very different indeed from their parent.

Lewis F. Day, a fellow-member of the Art Workers' Guild, a designer who had worked very closely with Morris in the Arts and Crafts Movement, and as an examiner at South Kensington, gives us a critical view of Morris's work in printing, in his excellent monograph, published as the *Easter Art Annual* for 1899.

'It is a question whether his books would not have gained by less luxurious ornamentation. His page is sometimes overladen, and the repetition even of the beautiful borders in the *Chaucer* begins to weary you before you get to the end of the volume. One feels too that some of the brush drawn detail of the ornament, nobly as it is designed, is not delicate enough for the pages of a book, even when the type is as manly as the printer's own.

'In devising his types, Morris did a real service to typography. Printers generally will no doubt persist in wanting rather lighter type than his; but they cannot help learning from him: he has demonstrated not only the poverty of modern type, but how much better it can easily be made.'

It is impossible to look at the work of the other presses which rapidly came into being around the same time, or to read of the activities of publishers and designers in the succeeding twenty years, without being aware of the great influence Morris exerted even in cases where the product was so unlike his own in style.

In January 1913 appeared the first issue of *The Imprint*. Aimed at the trade, designers, artists, and indeed all interested in good printing, it has no stylistic resemblance to any Kelmscott book, although its affinities with the Doves Press and Essex House Press product are fairly clear. But on page ii of its Introductory Notes is a paragraph which places it exactly in its true function as a link between old and new, between Arts and Craft and Modern Movement.

'The Kelmscott Press, the Doves Press, and the Ashendene Press have done a great deal towards bringing about a Renaissance of Printing, and though the commercial printer is prone to speak slightingly of private presses, much of the improvement in his own work, especially in the design of the types he uses, is to be derived from this source. For our part we shall always be glad to notice and review, or in cases of special interest to reproduce, typical specimens of the work of private presses and amateur printers who attain a workmanlike standard of technical execution.'

The producers of *The Imprint* were admirers of Morris, who expressed their respect for his work not only in verbal references, but in the most practical way. The journal was printed in the specially designed Imprint type.

'The newly designed type in which our pages are presented to the reader was cut by the Lanston Monotype Company at our instance. We are exceedingly pleased with it, and congratulate the Monotype Company on having produced the finest face that has been put upon the general market in modern times. Its compeers among privately owned types – the very best of them – will find it bear any comparison. Mr. Duncan has indeed added a fine feather to his cap in producing it. Though cut for *The Imprint*, it is on sale to the general public; we have made no attempt to tie it up; for our policy is sincerely to improve the craft of which we are so proud. The type has been christened IMPRINT OLD FACE.'

The first article in this influential journal was by Lethaby, who in true Morris fashion wrote on 'Art and Workmanship'. In the course of the article occurs a passage, a useful pointer to the nature of Morris's influence, however unfashionable his forms might become.

'It cannot be doubted, however, that we might lead in the domestic arts, and this is shown by the great interest which foreign observers take in the English arts and crafts movement. The Germans, indeed, who know the history of this development in England better than we do ourselves, realising its importance from an economic point of view, have gone so far as to constitute a special branch of political economy which shall deal with the subject. One university, I believe, has established a professor's chair in the economics of arts and crafts. English study of fine lettering has in Germany been put into types which English printers are hastening to buy.'

The very interest in the provision of new typefaces which Morris had stimulated, the example he had given of scrupulous attention to arrangement, and the teaching and example of men like Lethaby and Ashbee – his close admirers – brought into being a school of thought which seemed totally at variance with him. The criticism made by Lewis Day was sharpened by the new men. Stanley Morison, in his *Four Centuries of Fine Printing*, which first appeared in 1924, spells it out clearly and justly.

'The influence of Morris's work was enormous, but it is infinitely to be regretted that his enthusiasm for the Middle Ages led him to go behind the roman letter. The Golden type is his single contribution to its development, for which he might have done so much more had he not been under the spell of the incunable. The Kelmscott Master had not realised that, although black is the ideal colour for a gothic age, the roman letter with its finer contour demands a different colour, and can be brought into conformity with gothic standards only by compromising its essential grace and form. So Morris's Golden type is coarse and heavy in comparison with that of, say, Tory. Yet the present generation of amateurs and practitioners of typography owes Morris a greater debt than is represented by the great Kelmscott *Chaucer* and his other books. Morris's work . . . powerfully recommended printing to the interest of the public, and thus the trade was stimulated almost against its will.'

That last comment might well be applied not only to Morris's effect on the printing trade, but to every activity in which he became involved. Morison's own typography is classical in character, refined and often severe, unemphatic and unrhetorical; and for him it is not simply the excess of ornament but the robustness of the type and the blackness of the ink which are blemishes. But he – like Lewis Day – while making the particular criticism, understands clearly how Morris was important as a printer: not stylistically, but in his concept of principled work.

Ten years after Stanley Morison's comments, Holbrook Jackson read a paper on Morris's typography, which opens with words which are a paraphrase (did Jackson know this as he wrote?) of a sentence in Morris's *Dream of John Ball* – 'William Morris is an ironic figure. His achievements not only missed their mark, but hit marks they were not aiming at. The master-pieces of the Kelmscott Press which he aimed at making "useful pieces of goods" were typographical curiosities from birth, and so far removed from the common way of readers that they have become models of what a book should not be. . . . The Kelmscott books are overdressed. They ask you to look at them rather than to read them. You can't get away from their overwhelming typography, and even if you could, you might still be cheated of your author by their highminded purpose, for in addition to being the creations of an impressive genius the Kelmscott books were protests against the logical conclusions of mechanical book-production. . . . But, in spite of many extravagances and some few absurdities, the Kelmscott influence has been beneficial.'

In the same centenary year, G. D. H. Cole, writing the introduction to the Nonesuch Press selection from Morris's writings, said of Morris's other work, that although a good deal of it dates, 'it is important as a landmark in the history of modern craftsmanship and design rather than for the positive pleasure it still has power to give. In printing, for example, Morris did wonderful work at the Kelmscott Press, and every fine modern printer is in his debt. But of his types, the "Troy" is over-elaborate; and only the "Golden" is really a type to be *read* with pleasure now.'

Gerald Crow, in *The Studio* centenary volume on Morris, makes the same qualification with regard to Morris's typography as the rest. He considers that his achievement was 'more conspicuously that of having awakened general interest in the production of volumes beautiful in every feature (including an appropriate type and an insistence upon well-proportioned margins) than of having contributed to type design as an independent art.'

Now that we no longer find it necessary to deride the Victorians as monsters, as pompous hypocrites, or as comic figures – though they, like us, were all these things and many others – we are better able to assess the worth of what Morris did because we are better able to assess its context.

What then was the history and the achievement of Morris's 'little typographical adventure' as he called his starting the Kelmscott Press in a letter asking William Bowden to come and work for him?

The press was founded in 1890. The first trial page – using Morris's own newly designed type – was pulled January 31, 1891, and the first completed book – *The Story of the Glittering Plain* – issued on May 8. But Morris had already entertained the first project of this kind as long before as 1868, while working on *The Earthly Paradise*. Burne-Jones was to illustrate the book, which was to be a large folio printed in double columns. Many illustrations were actually drawn, and forty-four of those for the story of *Cupid and Psyche* engraved – in a style rather different from the current wood-engraving style of the Dalziels or Swains, and owing a good deal to that of the later fifteenth century. George Wardle, George Campfield (the firm's foreman), Charles Faulkner, and Jane Morris's sister Elizabeth began the engraving; but Morris, as Wardle later told Mackail, swept them away to do them himself; he cut more than thirty of them. Specimen pages were set up; but the project came to nothing.

Again during the period 1871–2, while Morris was working on *Love is Enough*, he projected an illustrated edition, for which Burne-Jones made one drawing, and Morris designed a number of initials and ornaments – very close in character to the illuminated ornament of the manuscript poems he had recently completed for Georgiana Burne-Jones. Again, trial pages were set and pulled; and again the venture came to nothing.

It was not until 1888 that Morris again gave thought to the idea of designing printed books, although he wrote and illuminated several. He became friendly with a Hammersmith neighbour, Emery Walker, partner in a photo-engraving business, and infinitely learned in all things to do with printing. Walker's lecture to the Arts and Crafts Exhibition Society in November 1888 seems to have been the occasion which settled for Morris that the only way to get the sort of book he wanted was to print it himself; but he had already resumed the interest he had shown earlier, for his romance, *The House of the Wolfings*. It had appeared only a week or so after Walker's lecture and had been printed at the Chiswick Press under the author's supervision. Morris had had the printer use the Basle type (an early-nineteenth-century recutting of a sixteenth-century original) for the trial pages of 1868; and this was the type used for the new book. The title-page is set in caps, including several lines of verse; and the effect is very different not only from that of other commercially printed books of the time, but from that of the Kelmscott books which followed. They did not follow immediately. A year later Morris published *The Roots of the Mountains*, in which the experiments of *The House of the Wolfings* were carried further. Morris was enormously pleased with this book, calling it, Cockerell says, the best-looking book since the seventeenth century. It is not necessary to go so far as that; but it was a landmark in Morris's work. From now on, he must print himself.

He set to work to design a typeface, taking as models those of the earliest users of a roman face, and of these chose, finally, that used by Nicolas Jenson in his *Pliny* of 1476. Using photographic enlargements, he drew and redrew until he had the forms to his liking; and by the end of the year the cutting of the fount, by Edward Prince, was almost complete. Printing began with trial pages early in 1891, and the first book appeared on May 8. This first type Morris called Golden, after the *Golden Legend* of Jacobus de Voragine, which he intended to print as his first book; it took so long in finishing, however, as to be only the seventh. The second half of 1891 was busy with the designing, cutting, and casting of a new type, the Troy, a semi-blackletter, based on the types of Jenson's German contemporaries. This type was cut in a smaller size, for the printing of the *Chaucer*, from which it took its name. Morris began the design of a third type, basing this on an original used by Sweynheym and Pannartz at Subiaco; but it was not cut.

Many of the Kelmscott books have decorated initials and borders, and these Morris designed continuously during the last six or seven years of his life: six hundred and forty-four borders and initials, title-pages, inscriptions, and printers' marks. Illustrations for the Kelmscott books were by Burne-Jones, who did eighty-seven pictures for the great *Chaucer*, by Walter Crane, C. M. Gere, and Arthur Gaskin.

Since Morris's object in becoming a printer was to have complete creative control, he not only designed his own types, but had paper and ink made to his own specification.

Morris died in October 1896. There were several books in preparation, and these were completed; the Kelmscott Press then ceased to exist. But it had called into being several others, and inspired men like Charles Ricketts, St John Hornby, Lucien Pissarro, C. R. Ashbee, and Cobden-Sanderson, to work in the same spirit as Morris, although in terms of style they differed a good deal from him, as from each other.

It is by looking at the varied styles of these presses, rather than by concentrating on the grand manner of the Kelmscott *Chaucer*, that we shall be able most justly to assess the nature of Morris's achievement.

The dilution of the Morris influence and the meaningless imitation of misunderstood design elements in such books have tempted many critics to lay all the blame for them at Morris's door. If Morris's production at his own press was entirely of one kind (and yet even within this there was variety) it does not mean that he saw this as the whole of printing. Are we really to think that at the end of a lifetime of eminently practical experience of mastering and designing for so many kinds of production, including printing; of hard thinking about the theory of those crafts; and after so concise and unequivocal an expression of basic typographical principles, Morris did not mean what he said, or that he did not understand his own theory, when he declared that a book could be beautiful by virtue of typography alone, and when he spoke of the designing of books as architectural?

The making of books at his own press was the great joy of Morris's last years. This does not mean that he thought no other kind of book should or could be made, or would be beautiful – or useful. He was not designing and producing books to be read on the train – although a Kelmscott book like *Dream of John Ball* can be read on the train with more ease than most paperbacks. He was producing books to be read at leisure, in one's home; and, in accordance with a Victorian habit not by any means confined to his own circle, as likely as not for reading aloud. This is a perfectly proper approach for a designer to make; it cannot invalidate other approaches, nor they it. He is often charged with neglecting to design and produce cheap books for mass-production; but to make this charge in respect of an activity which was taken up primarily for his own pleasure is surely unreasonable. If he had set out with such an intention, he would certainly not have produced books in this style – nor can the Kelmscott style be assessed simply by looking at the black and white pattern on the surface of the paper; the matter is more involved than that. If we want to criticise him in the field of printing we must look at *The House of the Wolfings* and *The Roots of the Mountains*. These two books were produced for the market, published in the ordinary way, and printed commercially. Morris went to the best printer for the printing of these books; to the same who had set and pulled the trial pages of his two earlier ventures. Even before he came into contact with Emery Walker – from whom certainly he learned much – he looked at the work of living printers with discrimination.

A look at the title-page, and a text page, of *The House of the Wolfings* will show how he thought about the problems of printing books for the ordinary market. A look at the equivalent pages of *The Roots of the Mountains* will show the same characteristics and the same principles at work. Let us judge Morris by these two examples as well as by the books of the Kelmscott Press; let us remember the essential differences between the two spheres of action, and we shall make better sense of his otherwise inexplicable power to effect a revolution in typography and book design – a power generally acknowledged, but treated as if it were that of a shaman or conjurer. One other point ought to be made in this connection. It is often said that the

Kelmscott books were expensive; an examination of the list and description of the productions of the press made by Sydney Cockerell shows that several of them cost only thirty shillings; two books were published at seven and sixpence, two others at ten shillings; and that Morris's own lecture, *Gothic Architecture*, was actually published at a half-crown! Bearing in mind the substance and quality of the books, the perfection of production, and comparing these with the prices of commercially produced books, one sees that the charge is by no means true.

Morris's first book had appeared in 1858. It was printed at the Chiswick Press, where four years before the revived Basle type, cut by William Howard, had been used. When in 1868, Morris was projecting his fine edition of the then uncompleted *Earthly Paradise*, he went to the Chiswick Press for trial pages, and these were set in the Basle type. In the latter part of 1888, the printing of *The House of the Wolfings* was put into the hands of the same press; and whatever part, large or small, Morris may have played in the design of the trial pages of 1868, there can be no doubt that he played a considerable – and often an exacting – part twenty years later. In seeing the new book through the press, Morris began 'to learn something about the art of typesetting'.

Most typographers would consider the line overlong; but in respect of his regard to the whole-ness of the page opening, the treatment of margins, the solid setting, and the complete absence of any ornament, Morris is here working exactly to his principles of unadorned typography (apart from the use of the same setting for the ordinary and the large paper editions – which taught him that this was bad design). The principles of the Kelmscott Press were thus established in the course of his participation in good commercial printing – not reached out of the air. And the result of Morris's close supervision of *The House of the Wolfings* is a handsome book, pleasant to handle, and easy to read in spite of its length of line.

Having looked at these 'ordinary books' we should see to whom this particular aspect of Morris was directly transmitted. His influence was not transmitted abstractly by people who read his declared principles – and reversed his practice. Of his own time, the Doves Press is the one whose products are usually contrasted with the Kelmscott books. It might be said that here the dominant hand is Emery Walker's; that with Walker and Cobden-Sanderson in their uneasy but creative partnership, no credit need be given to Morris. It is doubtful whether either of the two would have agreed to such an exclusion of Morris's influence; one might even suggest that the very austerity of the Doves Press arose from the need to detach themselves from his long shadow. But rather than the Doves Press, let us look at C. R. Ashbee's Essex House Press and his Guild of Handicraft. There is no doubt about Ashbee's discipleship.

The Guild of Handicraft had already published a number of books; but immediately upon the closure of the Kelmscott Press, Ashbee bought one of the Albion presses and took on some of the craftsmen, in order to set up the Essex House Press. Whatever there may have been of sentimental homage in this, and certainly there was an important element of homage, there was also the sound practical reason that to maintain Morris's standards with craftsmen who had worked under his direction and understood his aims would be more sure than if he had to start again from the ground. Certainly, there is no case here of a general pervasive influence mysteriously producing results quite other than those of Kelmscott, but the intentional continuation of the work Morris had done there. But, in Ashbee's case, the product was differently directed. Yet even that difference of direction came straight from Morris.

Ashbee's own later type designs were unsuccessful; but in the first books from the new press, using Caslon Old Face, he achieves the simplicity and monumentality one has a right to expect from the application of Morris's ideas to a folio conceived in the terms of *The Roots of the Mountains* rather than of the Kelmscott *Chaucer*. From being printed at a hand press, on a substantial handmade paper, damped for printing, the Caslon type naturally presents a more solid and Morrisian appearance than if printed on a smooth mechanically finished paper. Ashbee followed Morris in the use of a truly black ink; in spite of modern strictures on this, a true black does make for greater legibility as well as for richer colour, although if one is using an ill-conceived type, the contrast of black and white on good paper will bring out its faults and make one more painfully aware of its particular illegibility.

The *Cellini* is a handsome, well-printed, legible book; it has no stylistic likeness whatever to the Kelmscott *Chaucer*; it is none the less directly based on Morris's principles and derives from his practice. If we turn from the Essex House Press to the Doves Press, we find a greater austerity and chaster use of type. The type itself, the Doves type, is strictly in the Morris tradition. It was cut by the same punch cutter, Edward Prince, who had cut the Troy and Golden types. It was based, like the Golden, on an early Venetian type used by Jenson; Jenson's *Historia Naturalis* of 1476 was the precise model from which the drawings were made for it, under Walker's supervision, and it was Morris's own copy that was used. Emery Walker, perceptive and critical, needed little guidance from Morris in printing matters; rather the contrary. Morris turned to him for detailed knowledge of the trade; but they had worked together for seven years in bringing into being and carrying on the Kelmscott Press. The influences here are mutual, but we may doubt whether Emery Walker or Cobden-Sanderson would, without Morris's example, have entered the world of the private press.

If we turn to the Ashendene Press, we find the same intimate connection between St John Hornby's practice and Morris's in the matter – the essential matter! – of the form and use of type. The Ashendene Press was founded in 1894, due directly to Morris's influence. St John Hornby used several different types, beginning with Caslon, then using the Fell types of the Oxford University Press; then, in 1900, his own, the Subiaco, in which the folio *Dante* is set. Subiaco, described by Bernard Newdigate as 'a Roman type with many Gothic features', derives from that used by Sweynheym and Pannartz at Subiaco, where they set up the first press on Italian soil. They printed for Italian humanists in this type which stands half-way between the first Gothic-derived letters and the Romans that were to supersede them everywhere in Western Europe. With its longer ascenders and descenders, the Subiaco gives a lighter page than Morris's Troy; it is also more condensed and sharper in detail, while its caps are roman, not Gothic. It is, with all these points of difference, of the same family as the Troy and Chaucer. One might say it was directly begotten by Morris, for it was a modern version of the same type that he had worked on during 1892–3. Hornby was completing what Morris had begun.

Ricketts's Vale Press type, Lucien Pissarro's Brook type, Herbert Horne's Montallegro, Florence, and Riccardi types, Douglas Cockerell's Ewell type were all based, following Morris, on the Venetian types of the late fifteenth and early sixteenth centuries. When *The Imprint* appeared, in January 1913, it was printed in a new, specially designed face – an Old Face – Imprint, cut and cast by the Lanston Monotype Company. Shanks had already put their Dolphin – another Old Face – on the market. By 1914, in fact, Morris's example, not merely his precept, had penetrated not simply through the 'taste' of 'progressive' printers, but, what is more important, through the activity of commercial typefounders; into the realm of machine-setting, not just that of hand-setting. Morris-derived types, as well as his example and ideas, were now generally available to the trade.

In the United States, where Morris's work had already had a considerable although not always good influence in the 1890s, Theodore de Vinne and Bruce Rogers (who bought the second of the Kelmscott Albion presses) with the Renner and Montaigne types, respectively, produced further variants; Goudy's Kennerley was put on the English market by Caslon.

In Germany and Austria the influence of the English Arts and Crafts Movement was profound. In the fields of fabric and wallpaper design, interior decoration and furnishings, English and Scottish models found many enthusiastic followers. In typography the influence was no less. Indeed, in important respects it may even have been greater in this field than in any other, for the most modern-minded of German designers had become impatient of the limitations and illegibilities of their traditional Fraktur types, so that they welcomed the English influence as an aid in making German art international. Designers like Behrens and Koch, Tiemann and Kleukens all worked, in the first years of this century and the closing years of the last, towards this momentous typographical revolution. Their first inspiration was from the English revival of calligraphy; the focus this gave on letter forms, decorative values, page structure, demands of legibility, was particularly valuable to them whether they were working to redesign Fraktur types, or seeking to overthrow them. They were influenced to an extent which has since been forgotten, by the many-sided nature of the Arts and Crafts Movement, of which the restoration of printing was at first a part. It was decades before the Roman types could win precedence over the Fraktur. In the long process, these German and Austrian designers – alongside the Belgian Van de Velde – made important international contributions; not least because, very early, the typefounding industry saw the value of what they were doing. The new typography in Germany thus became something of immediate commercial consequence. Its exponents were in no doubt that they were in debt to William Morris.

7 The Arts and Crafts Movement

The 1870s saw the firm establishment of Morris's reputation, and the full extension of the work of the firm, signalised by the taking of the Oxford Street showrooms in 1877, and the move to Merton in 1881. Printing apart – which alone among Morris's design activities was a personal venture – everything was gathered together at Merton. Production could go on there on a much larger scale, and Morris began to be able to delegate not only management but some of the design work. The firm's products began to be influential, not just among wealthy patrons and fellow architects and designers but also with the general public.

In the process of building the firm, Morris had achieved something else, not at first intended – a reputation as a master-craftsman. Without thinking of himself as other than an artist he had, by virtue of his own energy, his determination to control the product, and his adherence to the Pugin-Ruskin principle of truth to material, become not only accomplished and versatile but also an authority on half a dozen crafts. These he had restored, not merely in a technical sense but in the sense of bringing them back into reputable practice. He might have contented himself with a theoretical knowledge of the crafts and the direction of the work of others. But his essentially moral dislike of directing others to do what he could not do himself drove him to become the great exemplar of the craftsman-designers. He found like Pugin, that industry could not meet his standards of technique and production. Pugin ascribed this to moral degeneracy and lack of Christian faith. Morris's early sympathies with this idea were replaced in the 1870s by a much more far-reaching account of the decadence of the crafts; but his debt to Pugin's example is real even although he made more of his debt to Ruskin's ideas.

He may well have received a different impulse from his rigorous days in Street's office, where he can never have taken part in actual design work. Street shared with Pugin an extraordinary facility in execution; with an abnormally accurate visual memory and fantastic skill, he could produce in two hours what would have taken any of his assistants a week. Norman Shaw, who followed Webb as Street's chief clerk, said that he did not think that he had, while working for Street, designed so much as a single moulding. A limitation as total as this must have been intolerable to Morris. No wonder that, in constant contact with the exuberant brilliance of Rossetti, he gave up architecture for painting, in which, however inadequately, his hands daily brought into being forms to embody his imagination.

Morris's interest in and practice of the crafts was not by any means unique. Pugin had set up his private workshop; James Brooks, the devout Anglican master of Mackmurdo, believed that an architect should know all about the crafts and their design down to the last hinge or door-knocker; Butterfield, Burges, Street, Seddon, Blomfield, painters like Eastlake and Madox Brown, all concerned themselves with design for crafts, and were all aware of the impossibility of getting the trade designers to produce anything tolerable. Watts, Leighton, and Herkomer all concerned themselves with more than one craft. But none of Morris's contemporaries was so versatile as he was. None combined as he did a supreme power of design with the running of a successful manufacture – using the word in its literal sense – in which design, production, and quality were all under his complete control.

Had he merely thought of himself as an individual craftsman fighting single-handed the monster of industrial production, with the product of loom and kiln, he could not have made the mark he did; nor could he have survived. Had the dwindling of his early income from the Devon Great Consols Company not so nearly dried up as to compel him to make a viable business of the firm, he might well have remained in the 'Palace of Art' of whose seduction he was so well aware. The decorating and furnishing trades had to take notice of him because he did indeed teach them their business, and was successful in competition with them; fellow artists and designers had to take notice because of the uncompromising excellence of his work and the force of his example. Pugin had been eloquent; Ruskin had been eloquent; Morris too was eloquent, and his thought came largely from theirs; but his practice was his own, and his thought in consequence goes far beyond it. He ceased, very early, to be a mere Gothic Revivalist.

Lewis F. Day, whose political and social ideas were very different from his, but who was greatly influenced by his example, while deploring his aversion to the fruits of the Renaissance, said justly of him that 'in the end his mediaevalism was distinctly modern'. Day was speaking of the character of Morris's design; but the same is to be said of his ideas about design as an activity of society. His essential modernity comes out in the lectures given in the 1880s, when his manufacturing and political activities combined had compelled him to a more informed study and deeper analysis of the relation between art and society than had been possible for him – or anybody else – in his romantic early days. Nor were his earliest designs imitation Gothic; much less than any of his contemporaries did he seek that exact archaeological imitation for which the work of 1862 was praised by the Exhibition judges.

Although Morris never practised as an architect, it was his architectural concept of design, rather than his mastery as a craftsman, that made him so powerful an influence; and in this he is very much of his age. It is Morris's firm root in architecture that gives long-term sense and coherence to his craft activities. Too often his work is looked at in terms of his life-long friendship with Burne-Jones; while the importance of this friendship, and its genuinely creative force, are not to be ignored, the almost equally long connection with Philip Webb is more significant. Webb and Morris were not simply friends and collaborators; they were both a part of the most creative movement in architecture of their time; a movement arising from but not to be confused with the Gothic Revival. And it is from the architects, rather than the designers or artists, that the mainstream of development flows. It is for his influence on architects who are interested in the whole field of design, much rather than for his influence on artists or designers, that Morris is important and contributes so much to the foundations of modern design.

This is apparent when we look at the Arts and Crafts Movement so closely associated with him. Although men like Walter Crane, Selwyn Image, Lewis F. Day, Henry Holiday are important figures, the most significant are those whose roots, like Morris's, are in architecture. Even in the founding of the various bodies which sprang into being to promote the recognition of the craftsman and designer, it was the architects who played the most important part. Mackmurdo and Horne of the Century Guild; Voysey, Ashbee and his Guild of Handicraft; Baillie Scott, Mackintosh, Godwin, Norman Shaw, Blomfield, Lethaby not only played an important part in making the most memorable houses and public buildings of the century, but also in the great attempt at the reunification of all the arts. This powerful drive, originating in the English Gothic Revival, spread to the Continent in the 1890s. The Arts and Crafts Movement is not to be regarded as the work of woolly-minded cranks; through it, for a quarter of a century, British design became the great growing point. Out of it came the fundamental concepts of design for the modern world. Morris was the centre of this movement and was acknowledged not only in England in his immediate circle, but in Europe and North America.

The Arts and Crafts Movement may be thought of with all the generality implied by that term – 'movement'; but if it is examined in terms of its constituent parts, it sheds its misty mantle and becomes intelligible in the context of a study of twentieth-century, as well as nineteenth-century design.

The story of the Arts and Crafts Movement is a mixture of personal and collective efforts. The participants did not all share the same objectives or tastes; but all were united in the desire to see the designer raised to a status equal with that of the 'fine' artist and the architect, and to see well-designed goods of every kind made available to all levels of society.

The real story is one of many strands, and the most useful way to deal with it is by picking out individuals and showing how they contributed to a surprisingly well-concerted general movement.

Two such individuals were Arthur Heygate Mackmurdo and Christopher Dresser. The first was closely associated with Ruskin and with Morris. The second was antagonistic to Ruskin and never had any close association with Morris; he was indeed a little out of the main current, and yet he can now be seen as one of the pioneers of modern product design.

Mackmurdo worked for James Brooks, a Gothic Revival architect in the Ecclesiological tradition, who hesitated to take a pupil because of his belief that all his work should truly be the work of his own hands; and this included the design of furnishings. As a result, Mackmurdo began to study the crafts and to design wallpapers, furniture, metalwork, and embroidery. In 1874 he went to Italy as Ruskin's travelling companion, and stayed there for two years, shedding his Gothic predilections in favour of the Renaissance, and making collections of traditional design. In 1875 he set up in partnership with Hornblower and Walters, whose chief practice was in Lancashire; and in 1880, after a second visit to Italy, he set up workshops of his own with the help of his pupil Herbert Horne.

Two years later he founded the Century Guild – which initially at least was simply a new name for Horne and himself in their joint capacity of designers for the crafts; however, other artists and designers joined with them, and the *Hobby Horse*, a magazine of the arts and crafts, was begun. Mackmurdo himself produced and designed the first issue, which he showed with pride to William Morris with whom he had come into contact as a designer, as an architect, and as a member of Anti-scrape. The work of the Guild designers was partly produced in their own workshops, but very largely by commercial firms. Wallpapers were printed by Jeffery and Company, fabrics by Simpson and Godlee of Manchester, and furniture made by Goodall of Manchester. The Guild showed work at many exhibitions, and stylistically much of it heralds the work of the 1890s and of Art Nouveau. Mackmurdo also founded the Home Arts and Industries Association, was very active in promoting art in general education, and published the Fitzroy Prints – large reproductions of specially designed drawings made for school use by such artists as Heywood Sumner. It was Mackmurdo who introduced Frank Brangwyn to William Morris – having encountered him as a youth painting in the City: as a result Brangwyn worked for Morris for some years and, although his reputation was made as a painter, it seems more likely to revive in terms of the more limited but very fine designs he made for furniture.

The Century Guild was never a self-contained concern like the Morris firm; nor an all-embracing organisation like the Art Workers' Guild; but it influenced many designers of a new generation, and was one of the sources of the Art Workers' Guild and the slightly later Arts and Crafts Exhibition Society.

Christopher Dresser, a devout admirer of Owen Jones, and a very serious analyst of design, was one of the early products of the National School of Design. For many years he lectured on botany at the School of Design, at the new Polytechnic Institution, and at the Crystal Palace. He published books on design, and probably had more influence among the craftsmen than the designers. He worked also for industry, designing wallpapers and cretonnes and interiors – often rather ineptly. But his great and permanent contribution was his work in design analysis of metalwares, glass, pottery, and other three-dimensional products; in which his consideration of mechanical function was reinforced by his study of Japanese design – not just of prints and ornaments, but of craft objects. Although some of the earlier and more theoretical designs look odd today, he came to be a most accomplished designer in this field, and his thinking anticipates much twentieth-century work.

As a result of this activity, in 1880 he set up the Art Furniture Alliance, with a showroom and shop in New Bond Street, where metalwares, pottery, glass, and fabrics, chiefly to his own designs, were displayed and sold. His designs for glass, and some of his metalwares, were truly original and good; his furniture was often rather doctrinaire and cranky, but came in some ways close to the more subtle and elegant work of E. W. Godwin, designer of Whistler's White House, who was also influenced by Japanese work.

Japanese design also became familiar to the general public through a number of shops, of which Liberty's was by the end of the century the best known. Liberty himself was not a designer, and it was not until his shop was well established that he began to commission designs. The new movement in design had now established itself. Liberty added to his stock of Japanese, Chinese, and Indian goods rugs from the Middle East; embroidery and lace from Greece and Malta and eventually modern home-designed fabrics, choosing first-rate designers such as Godwin, Voysey, and Alan Vigers. As soon as he embarked on this policy, he found, like Pugin and Morris before him, that the trade simply could not work to high standards. Like them, therefore, he did what he could to get the best work out of a small number of chosen firms, but in the end he set up his own print-works – near those of Morris, at Merton – in order to control the production of the silks and furnishing fabrics for which his shop was becoming internationally famous.

Some manufacturers also realised the importance of good design, and employed designers of the new trend. Woollams in textiles, Jeffery in wallpapers, Turnbull and Stockdale in cottons, set an early example and Owen Jones, Crane, Day, designed for them. The idea that there was more to design than the deadly adaptation of existing patterns stolen from the French began to make some impression, and although the great bulk of production remained of that order, the last twenty-five years of the century found room for a good number of independent designers to maintain lucrative practice and win public, as well as professional reputation.

Mackmurdo's Century Guild, and its journal, the *Hobby Horse*, contributed directly to the founding of the Art Workers' Guild; and no account of nineteenth-century design – or indeed twentieth-century design – can be adequate which does not deal with this body. The Century Guild, however, was not the only tributary. In 1881 a group of designers, led by Lewis F. Day, began to meet regularly to discuss their work; calling itself The Fifteen, and generally numbering about that. It included Walter Crane, Henry Holiday, Hugh Stannus (who had worked with Alfred Stevens), and J. D. Sedding. A little later, another group of friends, this time archtiects, also began to meet, to discuss design and the general state of the arts. This group called itself the St George's Art Society. Most of its members were architects, pupils or former pupils of Richard Norman Shaw. After a number of meetings, it seemed to them good to open their membership to artists and designers; one of the major difficulties they saw in the way of a real revival of art and design was the narrow professionalism and exclusiveness of the Royal Institute of British Architects and the Royal Academy. Towards the end of 1883 a committee of five was deputed to consult with Norman Shaw and later made a report on the need for some sort of body which should bring together artists and designers of every kind.

'The drifting apart of Architecture, Painting, and Sculpture is shown on the one hand in the trade decoration of our buildings, and on the other in the subject painting and portrait sculpture of our Galleries. But any real Art-revival can only be on the lines of the unity of all the aesthetic arts.' So wrote Lethaby in a contribution towards the committee's report. Three schemes were put forward, of which Lethaby's came nearest to the nature of the society which was actually formed. The important difference between his proposals and those of Newton and Macartney was that he included all kinds of artists, designers, *and craftsmen* – 'actual workers in the minor arts' is his phrase: and the proposals go on to state as objects '(1) forwarding the cause of art and (2) helping Decorative Art, and especially restoring certain art handiworks now almost lost or entirely forgotten; (3) spreading a knowledge of principles among the several trades and among the public'.

The name the Art Workers' Guild was adopted and membership was defined by Rule 2 as 'Handicraftsmen and Designers in the Arts'. In January 1909, Selwyn Image, a former Master of the Guild and later Slade Professor at Oxford, gave an address on the twenty-fifth anniversary of the foundation. Claiming that the work of the Guild and its members had been responsible in that time for a great change in the minds of artists and the public about the nature of art – now seen as embracing every kind of design and work in crafts, and not to be only painting in oils – he says: 'How can I at this point refrain from mentioning by name one to whom the principle of this Guild was as the very breath of his nostrils, who devoted his enthusiastic strenuous life to the propagation of it – how can I refrain from mentioning the great, the venerable name of Past-master William Morris?' And by this time, Morris's name and that of the Art Workers' Guild were both widely known and respected.

The Guild consisted of designers who worked for the most part individually, in their own workshops, or for industry. They met regularly to discuss design topics; but their meetings were private and the body had, so to speak, no public face. Some of the members wanted to change this and make a great combined assault upon industry and the public. In part this was connected with the war conducted by the painters of the New English Art Club against the exclusiveness of the Royal Academy, and there were negotiations between members of the New English Art Club and the Art Workers' Guild for concerted action; but nothing came of this.

The idea of a large public exhibition, however, in which craft and design work should be shown on a level with the 'fine arts' was a logical outcome of their association, and in 1886 W. A. S. Benson began to work towards this.

Benson, an admirer and associate of Morris, had been trained under Basil Champneys, one of the architect founders of the Art Workers' Guild; but rather than practise as an architect, he had, through his association with Morris, set up workshops for the production of metalwares – including such novelties as electric light-fittings which embodied several interesting and totally un-Gothic ideas. Under the title *The Combined Arts*, a circular was sent out seeking support, and in the autumn of 1888, now under the name of the Arts and Crafts Exhibition Society, the first exhibition was held in the New Gallery, Regent Street. It is interesting that among the supporting names of artists and designers there also appeared those of Thomas Wardle and Metford Warner – the close associates and trade printers of Morris's chintzes and wallpapers respectively.

The first paragraph of the circular indicated clearly the aims of the new body:

'Something very like a revival of the arts and handicrafts has been taking place among us of late years: but while the awakening of interest is undeniable and widespread, there has hitherto been no means of enabling those concerned with the more purely artistic side of the applied arts, or crafts of design, to gauge our general progress. It has not been possible for a craftsman to test his work by the side of others, or, by careful selection of examples, to prove that there are artists in other ways than oil or watercolour, and other art than that enclosed in gilt frames or supported on pedestals. In short, there is no exhibition which gives an opportunity to the designer and craftsman as such to show their work under their own names, and give them at least a chance of the attention and applause which is now generally monopolised by the pictorial artist. . . .' And further '. . . Art exhibitions have hitherto tended to foster the prevalent notion that the term "art" is limited to the more expensive kinds of portable picture painting, unmindful of the truth that the test of the condition of the arts in any age must be sought in the state of the crafts of design.'

Although Morris took part in the work of the Arts and Crafts Exhibition Society, and his help and work were alike valuable, he had reservations about its possible success; and indeed about the desirability of the exhibition system at all.

The event proved Morris wrong; the exhibition and those that followed were very successful; so too were the lectures which were given while the exhibitions were held. Morris himself lectured on tapestry and, in later years, on textile design and Gothic architecture: while it was on the occasion of the first exhibition that Emery Walker gave the lecture on printing which is usually credited with having provoked Morris into the founding of the Kelmscott Press.

C. R. Ashbee, another architect, born in 1863, had been articled to G. F. Bodley, and spent some time living and teaching at Toynbee Hall in East London. In 1887 he started his School of Handicraft, and this gave rise to the Guild in the following year. The two closely connected enterprises were meant to train and to trade in craft and decorative work, and Ashbee was responsible for most, though by no means all designs. He was a very close follower of Morris at this stage, but his attempts to revive something like mediaeval guild conditions were rather *naïve*; he was an admirable designer of furniture and jewellery; but certainly much less business-like than Morris. After ten years the Guild was reconstituted as a limited liability company, and in 1902, unwisely as it proved, moved the workshops out of London to Chipping Campden in Gloucestershire; an area which Morris had considered before finally settling on Merton. Here a new School of Arts and Crafts was opened, which survived the liquidation of the Guild in 1908, by six years. Ashbee then returned to architecture, though he continued to design, and a number of the Guild craftsmen continued, setting up their own workshops.

Ashbee's ideas changed a good deal during the twenty-six years of this endeavour; the primitive, anachronistic notion of the craft guild supporting itself by making high-quality goods to order while growing its own food simply ran into bankruptcy, but the process made Ashbee think much harder about the nature of society and the use of machinery than he had done. Bitter experience taught him what Morris had already made clear in *News From Nowhere* and in a number of his lectures that the new society could only come about by the much-extended, but rationally applied use of machinery. 'Furthermore,' says Morris in *A Factory as it Might Be*, 'machines of the most ingenious and best approved kinds will be used when necessary, but will be used simply to save human labour.' The qualification as to their use is based not on limiting possible applications of the machine, but on limiting its social use – which, in Morris's socialist future, should not be for profitmaking.

Ashbee's importance lies very largely in his carrying this thought forward – though less clearly than Morris – and in the exhibition of his own furniture and metalwork in Vienna, Munich, and Brussels. Although Morris's name and work were known abroad, the actual objects which excited most curiosity were, certainly in the 1890s, those designed by Ashbee, Baillie Scott, and Mackintosh – the younger men of the movement, whose forms were less obviously based on historic design and had begun to be more arbitrary and abstract.

Another architect, of the same generation as Ashbee, a member of the Art Workers' Guild and an exhibitor with the Arts and Crafts Exhibition Society, was C. F. A. Voysey. Born in 1857, he was articled to Seddon, and began to practise in 1882. He designed extensively for industry, especially in textiles and wallpapers, developing a very marked personal idiom. Most of his fabrics were designed for Alexander Morton and Company, and most of the wallpapers for Essex and Company, although he designed for a number of other firms as well, including Liberty's. Many of these designs were reproduced and used in Austria and Germany, and his influence on the Continent, both as designer and architect, was very great. Stylistically, Morris must have found his work distasteful; yet Voysey was an undoubted disciple, and is one of the most significant bridges between Morris and our own times.

The connection with continental design was at its most complete in the work of Baillie Scott, an architect born in 1865, who worked in idioms close to Voysey's in the 1890s and early 1900s, both in building and in fabric, wallpaper, and furniture design. His most notable work was the complete scheme of decoration and furnishing of the Palace of the Grand Duke of Hesse, at Darmstadt, in 1898, the work for which was carried out by Ashbee's Guild of Handicraft. Baillie Scott wrote articles for *The Studio*, which, first published in 1893, had a very large international circulation and did a great deal to spread the influence of the Arts and Crafts Movement in Europe. The Darmstadt designs were written up and reproduced in the magazine, and, with the work of C. R. Mackintosh, designer of the remarkable new buildings for the Glasgow School of Art, excited very wide and deep interest among younger designers in Germany, Austria, and Belgium.

Work by English Arts and Crafts designers was shown in many continental exhibitions, and partly because of the growing abstraction of the forms used, presented itself as the type of the art of the new century. Stylistically, it was the work of this younger generation of Arts and Crafts men that was most stimulating to the continental designers, although Morris was recognised and revered as the great founder figure, and his work, and that of close associates such as Walter Crane, continued to be exhibited; forming, for example, the largest unit in the big exhibition in the Pavillon de Marsan, Paris, in 1914.

Last, although there were many more – and I have neglected the many individual craftsmen in favour of the more influential architects – of this generation, important not just for their work in architecture and design in this country, but equally important as influences on an international plane, mention should be made of W. R. Lethaby. One of the founders of the Art Workers' Guild and the Arts and Crafts Exhibition Society, pupil of Norman Shaw, Lethaby did not design many buildings. Of all the younger men, he came closest to Morris in his ideas – lecturing and writing in a terse, provocative style on art and architecture. As Head of the new Central School of Arts and Crafts in 1894, and later as Professor of Design at the Royal College of Art from 1900, he had a great deal of influence. The Central School realised the ideal that had lain behind the original founding of the School of Design in 1837, which had never succeeded in carrying out its intended purpose of equipping designers to work for industry. After sixty years, the work, example, and teaching of Morris and his associates had transformed the general situation, and the new school embodied the experience of the Arts and Crafts Movement. It became, if not the model, certainly the inspiration of much continental teaching and training in design and the crafts. It was based on the belief that the designer must learn the nature of his materials by the practice of his craft; on the belief in the unity of the arts within an architectural frame; on Morris's familiar injunction to 'have nothing in your houses that you do not know to be useful or believe to be beautiful'.

Lethaby was not only, of all these men, the one closest in sympathy to Morris; he was also the clearest headed and least sentimental, and the most capable of carrying the essence of Morris's thought logically into the twentieth century; something which may be very simply exemplified in his share in the founding, in 1915, of the Design in Industry Association.

The possibility of carrying Morris's thought forward rests upon two things: we must understand his belief in the necessity of art to human life – in everyday terms as well as in terms of special cases; and we must understand his ideas on the machine and social responsibility. We must also, of course, realise that these ideas are inextricably interwoven for him.

Art, for Morris, came more and more to mean the well-doing of what must be done, the excellent making of what we must or wish to make. It is essential to understand that for him the activity of making was critical; it was as important as the thing made, and much as he loved himself to do and to make, much as he treasured well-made and beautiful objects, it was as the embodiment of human thought, feeling, and action that these things were valuable. He had no conviction whatever of an abstract beauty existing outside the sphere of human action, except in the sense of nature as an inexhaustible source of forms. Just as he demanded that a pattern should embody something of the imagination, so he recognised that all design – pattern design and the design of objects alike – embodies history; embodies, too, something of the personality of the maker. The work of the designer and craftsman involves constant judgements. It is therefore a responsible activity, creative not only of things useful and beautiful, but of the maker himself. The mere subservience to machinery, which he saw as a characteristic of the industrial production of goods, far from creating personality, destroyed and deadened it. He saw the worker at the bench, lathe, and loom, reduced to an animated component of the mechanical process; dehumanised, robbed of responsibility, his innate creativity totally annulled – and this in the interest of producing articles inferior to what had formerly been made by hand. It was a condition of life he knew he would not tolerate for himself: why then should it be tolerated at all?

But this was not the whole of his thought on the machine. He knew very well that machine power was with the world to stay. He knew, too, that it would go on developing and being, in a technical sense, perfected. His second objection to the use of machinery, or rather, of a system in which the machine dominates (not at all the same thing) lay in the ends to which it was put. Firstly as to the kind of thing made, but secondly – and for him this became more and more the most important thing – the end beyond that making: which was profit. The pursuit of profit, not the well-making by modern means of making, he saw to be the dominant force in industry. To understand Morris fully on this subject, one must start with his reading of Carlyle and Ruskin, with their jeremiads against smoke and steam and the squalor of the new industrial age; of Dicken's *Hard Times* – a favourite among his early reading – and see this moral critique ordered and rationalised by his reading of Marx's *Capital* in the 1880s.

Morris never wrote any book or essay, or delivered any lecture, on the single question of the machine. This is perhaps a guide to the nature of his thought about it; it was not, contrary to what is usually said of him, the machine itself which he held in abhorrence as a thing unclean. It was its use and abuse which moved his hatred: it was the spectacle of the machine (meaning irresponsible industry as a whole) destroying men while it made things, regardless of use or beauty. Morris has been criticised for failing to address himself to the problem of the machine-product. The real machine-product appeared to him to be simply profit; all other objects that came from it to be incidental by-products; and to the question of profit he certainly addressed himself with tremendous energy and critical force.

What Morris had to say on the machine in the simple sense of the word has to be sought in many places among his lectures; it can also be found in his *News From Nowhere*. When found, it makes very clear that this Utopia, this dreamland, rests in fact on the necessary use of the machine and of applied power: it was Morris, not Henry Ford, who spoke of the real possibility of the hours of labour being reduced to as little as four a day – this already in the early 1890s!

Among the lectures in which he speaks of the use of the machine are: *How we live and how we might live*, *The beauty of life*, *Useful work versus useless toil*, and *A factory as it might be*.

One sample may reasonably serve for all – but it must be remembered that Morris's thought was not static; what follows is one of his earliest statements.

In *Useful work versus useless toil*, a lecture given to the Hampstead Liberal Club in 1884, he has this to say:

'As to that part of labour which must be associated on a large scale, this very factory system, under a reasonable order of things (though to my mind there might still be drawbacks to it) would at least offer opportunities for a full and eager social life surrounded by many pleasures. The factories might be centres of intellectual activity also, and work in them might be varied very much: the tending of the necessary machinery might to each individual be but a short part of the day's work. The other work might vary from raising food from the surrounding country to the study and practice of art and science. It is a matter of course that people engaged in such work, and being masters of their own lives, would not allow any want of foresight to force them into enduring dirt, disorder, or want of room. Science duly applied would enable them to get rid of refuse, to minimise, if not wholly destroy, all the inconveniences which at present attend the use of elaborate machinery, such as smoke, stench, and noise; nor would they endure that the buildings in which they worked or lived should be ugly blots on the fair face of the earth. Beginning by making their factories, buildings and sheds decent and convenient like their homes, they would infallibly go on to make them not merely negatively good, inoffensive merely, but even beautiful, so that the glorious art of architecture, now for some time slain by commercial greed, would be born again and flourish.

'Meanwhile, the refinement, thoughtfulness, and deliberation of labour must be paid for; but not by compulsion to labour long hours. Our epoch has invented machines which would have appeared wild dreams to men of past ages, and of these machines we have as yet made no use.'

A quotation from Lethaby's lecture on design and industry, given to the newly founded Design in Industry Association in 1915, will serve both as a sample of his extremely direct style and of his place as the bridge between Morris and modern times.

'The Arts and Crafts Movement of the last quarter of the century was also a specially English product which has been much studied and imitated abroad, while it has been allowed to struggle helplessly at home. With occasional extravagance and affectation it is certain that it produced ideas in plenty, ideas which in many cases have been taken up and worked by our foreign rivals.

'The difficulty has been that the designer and the manufacturer have so largely remained in separate compartments, and that the purchasing public had yet a third point of view. The political economist has preferred to dwell in another watertight compartment. As Adam Smith did not bother about design, why should he? He has, in fact, become an idealist of crude labour because he can deal with it mathematically. Quality, he finds, is a disturbing matter of opinion, so he tries to get rid of it by acting as if it were not there.'

After reminding his audience that continental manufacturers had learned from our Arts and Crafts Movement what our own manufacturers had signally failed to do, Lethaby goes on:

'The things of which we have been speaking have been produced in England by a special class of enthusiasts for a small number of connoisseurs, and the large manufacturer has not seen what great possibilities there were in adapting these experiments to the larger world of machine industry. Now this is just what our foreign competitors have done.

'Design is too often thought of as an inexplicable mystery, and it is difficult to get it understood that design does not necessarily mean a pattern drawn on paper, nor does it involve some strange originality; but it should be just the appropriate shaping and finishing for the thing required. . . . Design is not some curious contortion of form, or some super-added atrocity, but should rather be conceived of as the fitting of means to ends in the production of works which are good each in their own order.'

This is, of course, a demand for functional design; it does not exclude the design of ornament and pattern, as so many people came to think; pattern and ornament have their functions as Morris had well understood; and neither he nor Lethaby after him meant by function only mechanical efficiency. At the centre of the notion of function is the human activity or pleasure which the design must serve; a design may be generous and exuberant, or trim and austere – and in each case functional.

If Lethaby was the great link between English and European thinking on design, his German counterpart was Hermann Muthesius, with whom he was well acquainted. Muthesius was attached to the German Embassy in London from 1896 to 1903. His function was to research into English housing – and by logical extension into English design in general. The ideas which he took back to Germany were precisely those which Lethaby promoted and which were at the core of the work of the Central School of Arts and Crafts. In 1907 there was set up the Werkbund: similar organisations followed in Austria and Switzerland and in Scandinavia. German Schools of Art were reorganised on lines derived from Muthesius's English experience. Men like Peter Behrens in Düsseldorf, Van de Velde in Weimar, Bruno Paul in Berlin – architects deeply interested in design, and already independently stimulated by the English Arts and Crafts Movement – became their principals. When, in 1914, Van de Velde left the Weimar School, he nominated Walter Gropius as his successor. The appointment did not take effect because of the intervening war; but when in 1919 Gropius was able to take up his post, he reorganised the school as the Staatliches Bauhaus – and as the Bauhaus this school came to stand for all that was modern and forward-looking in design.

Gropius was in no doubt at all as to his lineage as a designer. He traces it clearly in *The New Architecture and the Bauhaus,* from Morris and the English Arts and Crafts Movement, through the Werkbund; and in the Bauhaus programme there is every kind of evidence of his close study of the work of men like Ashbee and Lethaby. Stylistically, the characteristic Bauhaus product was utterly alien to anything of Morris's own production; but it was made in his spirit.

The paradox is best expressed in the words of Morris's own *Dream of John Ball*:

'. . . *I pondered all these things, and how men fight and lose the battle, and the thing that they fought for comes about in spite of their defeat, and when it comes turns out not to be what they meant, and other men have to fight for what they meant under another name. . . .*'

Bibliography

Commencing with *The Defence of Guenevere*, published by Bell and Daldy in 1858, Morris published a considerable amount of work in separate volumes and some of his books were reprinted at his own Kelmscott Press. These works, with other unpublished material, were brought together in the *Collected Works* edited by his daughter May, who later supplemented the twenty-four volumes by two more under the title of *William Morris: Artist, Writer, Socialist*; and these twenty-six volumes form the main source of reference. The bibliography below is very far from exhausting the literature relating to the life and work of Morris; it simply lists the most useful source of published material. Unpublished material is to be found in the British Museum, The Victoria and Albert Museum, the William Morris Gallery, Walthamstow, The Bodleian Library; in the first three of which, and the Art Gallery, Birmingham, are also important collections of drawings and designs by Morris and his associates.

Morris's Own Writings
Briggs, Asa and Shankland, Graeme (ed)
WILLIAM MORRIS: SELECTED WRITINGS AND DESIGNS
Penguin 1962 Illustrated

Cole, G. D. H. (ed)
WILLIAM MORRIS: SELECTED WRITINGS
Nonesuch Press 1934

Henderson, Philip (ed)
LETTERS OF WILLIAM MORRIS TO HIS FAMILY AND FRIENDS
Longmans, Green & Co. 1950

Morris, May (ed)
THE COLLECTED WORKS OF WILLIAM MORRIS
Longmans 1910–1915 24 vols

Morris, May (ed)
WILLIAM MORRIS: ARTIST, WRITER, SOCIALIST
Basil Blackwell 1936 2 vols.

Books About or Relating to Morris's Life and Work
Arnot, R. Page
WILLIAM MORRIS: THE MAN AND THE MYTH
Lawrence and Wishart 1964

Crow, Gerald
WILLIAM MORRIS, DESIGNER
Studio 1934 Illustrated

Day, Lewis F.
WILLIAM MORRIS AND HIS ART
Easter Art Annual of the Art Journal 1899
Illustrated

Mackail, J. W.
LIFE OF WILLIAM MORRIS
Longmans 1899 2 vols

Thompson, E. P.
WILLIAM MORRIS: ROMANTIC TO REVOLUTIONARY
Lawrence and Wishart 1955

Thompson, Paul
WILLIAM MORRIS
Heinemann 1967

Vallance, Aymer
WILLIAM MORRIS: HIS ART, HIS WRITINGS AND HIS PUBLIC LIFE
George Bell 1897 Illustrated

Memoirs and letters of Morris's Friends and Associates
Birbeck Hill, G. (ed)
LETTERS OF DANTE GABRIEL ROSSETTI TO WILLIAM ALLINGHAM
T. Fisher Unwin 1897

Burne-Jones, Georgiana
MEMORIALS OF EDWARD BURNE-JONES
Macmillan 1904 2 vols

Crane, Walter
AN ARTIST'S REMINISCENCES
Methuen 1907 Illustrated

Doughty, Oswald
A VICTORIAN ROMANTIC: DANTE GABRIEL
ROSSETTI
Oxford 1949

Doughty, Oswald and Wahl, J. H. (eds)
LETTERS OF DANTE GABRIEL ROSSETTI
Oxford vols I & II 1965: vols III & IV 1967

Holiday, Henry
REMINISCENCES OF MY LIFE
Heinemann 1914 Illustrated

Hueffer, Ford Madox
FORD MADOX BROWN: A RECORD OF HIS LIFE
AND WORK
Longmans 1896 Illustrated

Hunt, William Holman
PRE-RAPHAELITISM AND THE PRE-
RAPHAELITE BROTHERHOOD
Macmillans Illustrated 2 vols

Jones, Owen, and Wyatt, Matthew Digby
THE GRAMMAR OF ORNAMENT
Day and Hague 1856

Lethaby, W. R.
PHILIP WEBB AND HIS WORK
Oxford 1935

Marillier, H. C.
DANTE GABRIEL ROSSETTI
George Bell 1899
Revised and abridged 1901 Illustrated

Millais, J. G.
LIFE AND LETTERS OF SIR JOHN E. MILLAIS
Methuen Illustrated 2 vols

Rossetti, W. M.
RUSKIN, ROSSETTI AND PRE-RAPHAELITISM
George Bell 1899

Books on design, decoration, art and architecture
Ashbee, C. R.
CHAPTERS IN WORKSHOP RECONSTRUCTION
Essex House Press 1894

Ashbee, C. R.
CRAFTSMANSHIP IN COMPETITIVE INDUSTRY
Essex House Press 1909

Ashbee, C. R.
WHERE THE GREAT CITY STANDS
Essex House Press and Batsford 1917

Crane, Lucy
ART AND THE FORMATION OF TASTE
Macmillan 1882

Crane, Walter
WILLIAM MORRIS TO WHISTLER
George Bell 1911

Crane, Walter
IDEALS IN ART
George Bell 1905

Day, Lewis F.
THE ANATOMY OF PATTERN
Batsford 1887

Day, Lewis F.
THE PLANNING OF ORNAMENT
Batsford 1887

Day, Lewis F.
THE APPLICATION OF ORNAMENT
Batsford 1888

Davison T. Raffles (ed)
THE ARTS CONNECTED WITH BUILDING
Batsford 1904

Dresser, Christopher
THE ART OF DECORATIVE DESIGN
Day and Sons 1856

Dresser, Christopher
PRINCIPLES OF DECORATIVE DESIGN
Cassell Petter and Galpin, n.d.

Eastlake, Charles L.
HINTS ON HOUSEHOLD TASTE
Longmans 1868 Illustrated

Garrett, Agnes and Rhoda and Jones, Owen
HOUSE DECORATION
Macmillan 1879 (6th ed)

Masse, H. J. L. J.
THE ARTWORKERS' GUILD 1884–1934
Artworkers' Guild 1935

Nikolaus Pevsner's *Pioneers of Modern Design* (Penguin 1960) Walter Gropius's *The New Architecture and the Bauhaus* (Faber 1935) and Peter Ferriday (ed) *Victorian Architecture* (Cape 1963) are all useful books.

In addition, journals such as *The Magazine of Art, The Art Journal* and *The Studio* contain much relevant material in the form of illustrated articles on art and design from the middle of the nineteenth century until 1914: by that date, the English lead in the field of design has run into the sand.

The Journal and other publications of the William Morris Society supply a continuing fund of information on new research into and re-examination of the work and ideas of William Morris, and will now always be necessary to any serious study.

General Index

Index of persons

1 *The Woodpecker* High warp tapestry designed by William Morris and woven in the 1880s. With the *Forest* tapestry woven for Alexander Ionides, it was shown in the first Arts and Crafts Exhibition 1888 *Courtesy, William Morris Gallery, Walthamstow, Essex*

2 3

4 5

6

2   Page of borders and patterns taken from mediaeval stained glass

3   Page of borders taken from mediaeval manuscripts

4   Page showing the supposed derivation of Egyptian painted ornament from the lotus plant

5   Page setting out the inherent geometry and order of natural forms. The abstraction and application of these forms was, for Owen Jones and Christopher Dresser (who drew this page), the essential work of the designer *'Grammar of Ornament', 1856, by Owen Jones*

6   Ceiling-paper designed by William Morris, showing influence of Persian decoration. Since a ceiling-paper must have no direction, this is made symmetrical about two axes and works on one plane only *Courtesy, Sanderson and Co.*

7 *Fruit* – or *Pomegranate* This was the third of the wallpapers Morris designed in 1864. Its naturalism ran counter to fashion, and its structure is in debt to tile work *Courtesy, Sanderson and Co.*

8 *Willow and Vine* An original drawing by Morris for a paper never put into production. Undated, it has the characteristics of the early 1870s when he resumed wallpaper design *Photo Dennis Frone. Courtesy, William Morris Gallery, Walthamstow, Essex*

8

9

9 *Blackthorn* Designed by Morris in 1892, this is a fine example of the bower-like effect he loved to make. Its symmetrical structure, based on weaving patterns, clothed with a variety of natural forms, asserts itself without dominating *Courtesy, Sanderson and Co.*

10 *Compton* The last of Morris's own wallpaper designs, produced in 1896 for Laurence Hodson's house of the same name. Perhaps the most perfect of his patterns in its combination of formal drawing and varied flow, it was also printed as a chintz *Courtesy, Sanderson and Co.*

10

11

12

11 *Vine* This pattern of 1873 belongs to the group of wallpapers Morris designed just before and just after taking over the firm in 1875. The firm drawing and dense organisation suggest the influence of the earliest block prints *Courtesy, Sanderson and Co.*

12 *Norwich* This paper, designed by Morris in 1889, is characteristic of the large-scale patterns suited to big and ceremonious rooms. Its diagonal meander comes from fifteenth-century design, and appears also in the *Wey, Cray, Wandle,* and *Trent* chintzes – all designs of magnificence made in the 1880s *Courtesy, Sanderson and Co.*

13 *Honeysuckle* by May Morris, who became responsible for the firm's embroideries in 1885. Most of her designs were for that medium, but she designed three papers, of which this is much the best; it is based, like many of her father's, on the vertical meander *Courtesy, Sanderson and Co.*

14 *Seaweed* by J H Dearle, makes an interesting bridge between the pure Morris style in which he grew up, and the exotics of Art Nouveau. It is one of his most successful, but his work was usually more like Morris's own *Courtesy, Sanderson and Co.*

15 *Birds* This double-woven wool fabric of 1878
was one of Morris's own favourites, and one of the
rooms at Kelmscott House, Hammersmith, was
hung with it. This detail is from a piece used as an
altar frontal in the Parish Church of St Margaret,
Rottingdean, Sussex *Photo J Thorpe*

16 *Dove and Rose* A silk and wool fabric designed
in 1879, this was also a favourite with the designer.
The original drawing is in Birmingham. *Photo
Dennis Frone. Courtesy, William Morris Gallery,
Walthamstow, Essex*

17

17 *Cray* This chintz was designed in 1885. Around this time, Morris named a number of chintzes after near-by rivers, perhaps because of their meander motif *Photo Dennis Frone. Courtesy, William Morris Gallery, Walthamstow, Essex*

18 *Eyebright* Indigo print on cotton. An unusual example of Morris working on a small scale pattern *Photo J Thorpe*

18

19

20 *The Flowerpot* Embroidered panel designed by
William Morris and worked in silk and gold on
linen by May Morris *Photo Dennis Frone. Courtesy,
William Morris Gallery, Walthamstow, Essex*

19 *The Romaunt of the Rose* Portion of the frieze
designed about 1872 by Morris and Burne-Jones
for Sir Lowthian Bell's house, Rounton Grange,
Northallerton, and worked in wool, silks, and gold
by Bell's wife and daughter *Photo Dennis Frone.
Courtesy, William Morris Gallery, Walthamstow,
Essex*

21, 22, 23   Windows, St Michael and All Angels, Brighton. This, G F Bodley's first church, was being built at the time of the founding of the firm and Bodley commissioned glass for it and a number of other churches *Photo J Thorpe. Courtesy, the Rector, St Michael and All Angels, Brighton*

21

22

23

24 Part of a window in the Parish Church of
Middleton Cheney, Northamptonshire, designed in
1864. Morris's own drawing for the figures of Eve
and the Virgin Mary is reproduced in fig. 51
*Photo Dennis Frone. Courtesy, the Rector, Parish
Church of Middleton Cheney*

25

25   Three-light east window, the Parish Church of
St Margaret, Rottingdean, Sussex. The Archangels
Gabriel, Michael, and Raphael are shown.
Designed by Burne-Jones and installed in 1893.
The church has several other Morris windows
*Photo J Thorpe. Courtesy, the Rector, Parish Church
of St Margaret*

27

26 *The Virgin Mary* Window in the Parish
Church of St Margaret, Rottingdean, designed by
Burne-Jones and executed by Morris and Co.
*Photo J Thorpe. Courtesy, the Rector, Parish Church
of St Margaret, Rottingdean*

27 *Self-portrait of William Morris* Probably
drawn while working in Street's office at Oxford,
under Rossetti's influence – it shows with what
difficulty he drew the human form *Courtesy,
Victoria and Albert Museum*

28 *William Morris c* 1890 This shows Morris as he
must have become familiar to thousands as
socialist propagandist and lecturer on art in the
1880s and early 1890s *Photo F Hollyer. Courtesy,
Robin Carruthers*

28

30   The entrance hall, Red House, showing the large cupboard painted by Burne-Jones and the undisguised structure of the staircase *Courtesy, 'Country Life'*

31   *Flamma Troiae* Drawing by William Morris *c* 1860–1 for embroidered hangings in the Red House. Portions of this embroidery, including this figure, are now incorporated in a folding screen in the Victoria and Albert Museum *Courtesy, Victoria and Albert Museum*

29   The Red House, Upton, Bexleyheath, Kent. This view taken within the angle of the building shows Philip Webb's personal use of a style already established by Street and Butterfield *Courtesy, 'Country Life'*

32

32 Cabinet designed by Philip Webb in 1862, and painted with scenes from the legend of St George by William Morris; his drawings for them and the cabinet itself are in the Victoria and Albert Museum *Courtesy, Victoria and Albert Museum*

33 Cabinet designed by Philip Webb *c* 1865, with panels painted by William de Morgan. The forward-curving hood is a typical feature of this sort of cabinet *Courtesy, William Morris Gallery, Walthamstow, Essex*

34 'Morris' Chair. This light, rush-seated chair, its woodwork painted black, was based on a traditional design found in Sussex by Warington Taylor. Sold for less than ten shillings even as late as 1914, they continued to be produced for nearly eighty years *Courtesy, Victoria and Albert Museum*

33

34

36

37

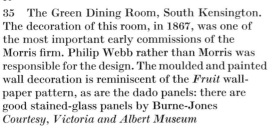

35 The Green Dining Room, South Kensington. The decoration of this room, in 1867, was one of the most important early commissions of the Morris firm. Philip Webb rather than Morris was responsible for the design. The moulded and painted wall decoration is reminiscent of the *Fruit* wallpaper pattern, as are the dado panels: there are good stained-glass panels by Burne-Jones *Courtesy, Victoria and Albert Museum*

36 Painted panel from the King René's honeymoon cabinet made for the architect J P Seddon in 1861. This panel by Ford Madox Brown depicts the art of architecture *Courtesy, Victoria and Albert Museum*

37 Painted panel from the Seddon cabinet by Dante Gabriel Rossetti. Panels by Burne-Jones depict sculpture and painting, and there are smaller square panels showing crafts such as pottery and weaving *Courtesy, Victoria and Albert Museum*

38 Bookcase and writing-desk designed by Richard Norman Shaw and made by James Forsyth. First shown in the Architectural Exhibition of 1861, and reproduced in *The Builder*, it was also shown in the Great Exhibition of 1862 *Courtesy, Victoria and Albert Museum*

39 Table designed by Augustus Northmore Welby Pugin. Gothic in character, it uses carved, not painted decoration. Pugin published many such designs and many were actually made *Courtesy, Victoria and Albert Museum*

40 Chairs designed and decorated by William Burges, *c* 1850 *Courtesy, William Morris Gallery, Walthamstow, Essex*

41 Chair designed by Arthur Heygate Mackmurdo early 1880s. The flame-like fretted ornament is typical of Mackmurdo and shows him as a precursor of Art Nouveau *Courtesy, William Morris Gallery, Walthamstow, Essex*

42 Writing-desk designed by A H Mackmurdo. Mackmurdo, unlike Morris, was an admirer of the Italian Renaissance, and his Century Guild furniture shows this *Courtesy, William Morris Gallery, Walthamstow, Essex*

38

39

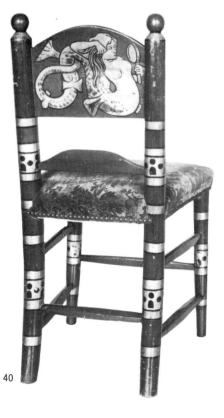

40

41

42

43

44

45

46

43 Tea service designed by Felix Summerly (Henry Cole). This design won an award from the Society of Arts in 1847, and was put into commercial production. It remained in favour for many years *Courtesy, Victoria and Albert Museum*

44 Plate designed by A N W Pugin for Minton and Co. Pugin, in addition to producing in his own workshops, designed a good deal for industrial firms like Minton and the Birmingham silversmith Hardman *Courtesy, Victoria and Albert Museum*

45 Chalice designed by William Burges for the Ecclesiological Society. Much church plate in the Gothic style was designed by architects like Pugin, Burges, and James Brooks, Mackmurdo's master, in the 1840s and 1850s *Courtesy, Victoria and Albert Museum*

46 Bookcase designed by A N W Pugin and made by Crace and Sons, the leading commercial furnishers and decorators of the mid-century. Its strictly architectural forms contrast with the flat panels, painting, and inlay of the next generation *Courtesy, Victoria and Albert Museum*

47

47 Sideboard designed by W R Lethaby. A pure
Arts and Crafts piece, this shows the search for a
style based on construction rather than historic
ornament; its architecture is its own *Courtesy,
Victoria and Albert Museum*

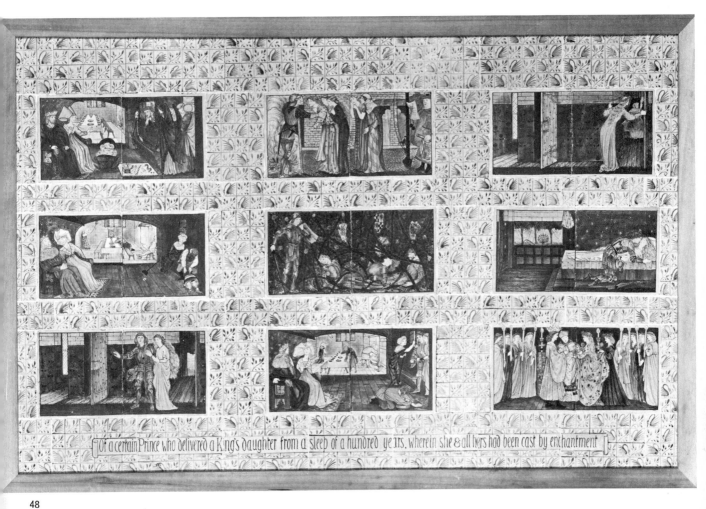

48 Tile panel from Birket Foster's house at
Witley, Surrey, 1864. The picture tiles are by
Burne-Jones, telling the story of Sleeping Beauty;
the blue and white pattern tiles, by Morris or
Webb, are painted, not printed *Courtesy, Victoria
and Albert Museum*

49 Design for stained glass, early 1860s,
St Michael and the Dragon, by Peter Paul Marshall,
about whom little is known, and of whose work
little survives *Courtesy, Victoria and Albert Museum*

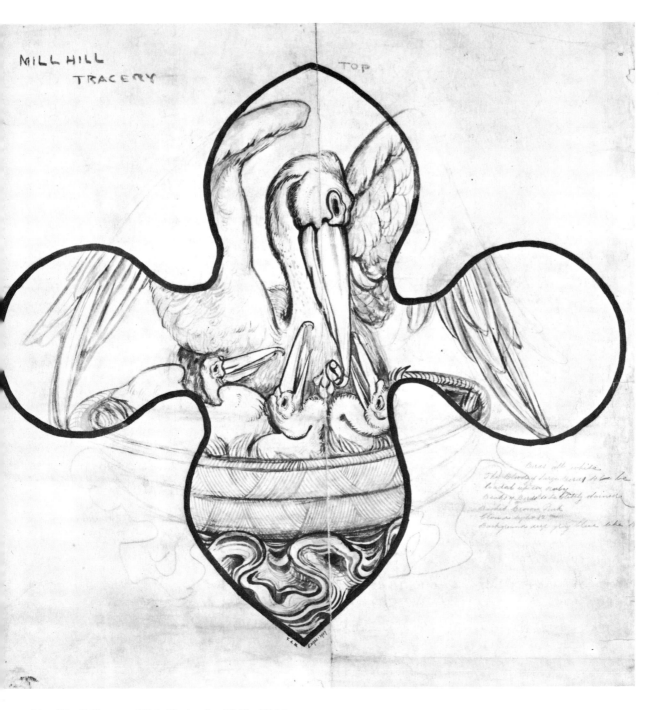

50 *The Pelican*, or *Piety* Design by Philip Webb
for stained glass. Webb was nearly always
responsible for the drawing of bird and animal
forms in the firm's glass, tapestry, and decoration
Courtesy, Victoria and Albert Museum

52

53

51 *Eve and the Virgin Mary* This drawing by
William Morris was made for the stained-glass
window in the Parish Church of Middleton Cheney,
in 1864. (Reproduced in colour fig. 24.) *Courtesy,
William Morris Gallery, Walthamstow, Essex*

52 Carpet designed by E T Parris for Turberville
Smith and Co., London, and exhibited in the
Great Exhibition of 1851. 'It is difficult to form
anything like a correct notion of the richness and
beauty of these fabrics', says the *Art Journal
Illustrated Catalogue* in which the carpet appears

53 Wilton carpet designed by William Morris
c 1880. This was machine-made by the trade as
distinct from the hand-knotted carpets and rugs
made by Morris and Co. at Hammersmith or
Merton Abbey *Courtesy, Victoria and Albert
Museum*

54

54 Hammersmith rug designed by William Morris and made at Hammersmith. The hammer and wavy line of these products was dropped when the work was transferred to Merton in 1881 *Courtesy, Victoria and Albert Museum*

55 Carpet designed by Morris in 1889 for the Sanderson house 'Bullerswood' in Kent. Hand-knotted, it is made with wool on a cotton warp *Courtesy, Victoria and Albert Museum*

56   *Rose and Lily* A silk and wool tissue designed by Morris in 1885; the colours are green, pink, indigo *Courtesy, Victoria and Albert Museum*

57   *Granada* Silk velvet in three colours with gold thread. Morris's only velvet, it was extremely costly. Designed in 1884, it is clearly based on fifteenth-century patterns *Courtesy, Victoria and Albert Museum*

58 Embroidered hanging for Rounton Grange worked in wool on linen by Margaret, wife of Sir Lowthian Bell *c* 1880 *Courtesy, Victoria and Albert Museum*

59 Working drawing for *Bluebell* chintz design by William Morris *Courtesy, Victoria and Albert Museum*

60 *Bluebell* Printed cotton (chintz) designed by Morris in 1876. Takes its name from the bluebell, which is sometimes printed in pink, rather than from the more obvious columbine, but is sometimes called *Colombine Courtesy, Victoria and Albert Museum*

59

60

61 *Honeysuckle*, 1876. This was a chintz of which Morris was rather proud both for its design and for the success with which its unusually large number of blocks were printed *Courtesy, Victoria and Albert Museum*

62 *Tulip and Willow* chintz, 1889. Morris here uses the same construction as in the earlier *Vine* wallpaper – a vertical meander throwing off scrolls to right and left *Courtesy, Victoria and Albert Museum*

63   *The Evenlode* chintz, designed by Morris in
1883, and taking its name from the river of that
name *Courtesy, Victoria and Albert Museum*

64   *Cherwell* This cotton velvet (velveteen) was
printed from Morris's design *c* 1885. The fabric was
not manufactured by the firm *Courtesy, Victoria
and Albert Museum*

65

66

Morris & Co. Queen Square

65 Gothic wallpaper, early nineteenth century, from a fragment in the Victoria and Albert Museum; hand-printed from wood blocks *Courtesy, Victoria and Albert Museum*

66 *Crystal Palace* wallpaper produced in 1852–3 by Heywood, Higginbottom and Smith; a comparable paper was produced by them on the occasion of the 1862 Exhibition. Hand-printed from wood blocks *Courtesy, Victoria and Albert Museum*

67 Morris and Co.'s record of wallpaper designs and blocks, kept by Jeffery and Co. who printed all the firm's papers until 1930 *Courtesy, Sanderson and Co.*

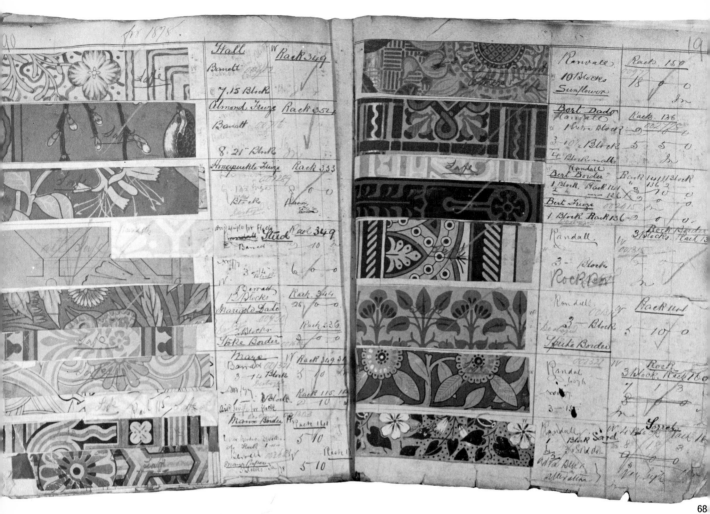

68 Page from Jeffery and Co.'s own records of blocks held by them for the printing of their own and other firms' wallpapers except Morris and Co. The small samples give some idea of the difference between the Morris papers and those in general production *Courtesy, Sanderson and Co.*

69 Page from Morris and Co.'s records of wallpaper blocks and colourings, kept by Jeffery and Co. It indicates changes of colourings, recutting of blocks, printings, etc *Courtesy, Sanderson and Co.*

No 86.
11.
Pimpernel
12 Blocks
002020
1st Set sent 22/9/76

C/a +10%
april 96

Now C/o for 50 pcs. 7/9/92
alt from 12 to 50
7/u for under 12 pcs
6/4 for 6 pcs for 92

No 87.
+1
Wreath
22 C.B.
002052
1st Set sent 27/9/76

A/d +10%
april 17/6

t/a 30 pcs 5/10/98

t/u 5 pcs 31/10/03
C/o for 9 pcs 27/5/91

16/. No 88
30. C.B. 002016
Acanthus
old price C/a (or /83)
1st Set sent 9/9/77

+10%
april 1916

69

71

72

70 *Daisy* wallpaper, 1864. One of the group of three papers first designed and produced by Morris, it remained popular throughout the firm's existence *Courtesy, Sanderson and Co.*

71 *Trellis* wallpaper, 1864. First designed of Morris's papers; the birds are by Philip Webb *Courtesy, Victoria and Albert Museum*

72 Working drawing for *Wild Tulip* wallpaper designed by William Morris in 1884 *Courtesy, Victoria and Albert Museum*

73

74

73 Working drawing by William Morris for the *Jasmine* wallpaper, 1872. One of the first designs produced when he resumed wallpapers in the 1870s, and one of his most original *Courtesy, Birmingham City Art Gallery*

74 *Scroll* wallpaper designed by Morris in 1871, before his interest in weaving and his preoccupation with historic ornament restricted the freedom shown here *Courtesy, Victoria and Albert Museum*

Scale
pattern

Wave
pattern

Lewis F. Day
1886

Feather
pattern

Ogee   pattern

Double
Ogee

Scale pattern & derivatives

75

75, 76, 77   Three pages from Lewis F Day's
Analysis of Pattern, a handbook prepared by him in
1886–7 for use in art schools; one of a series
published by Batsford. Illustrations like this were
used by Morris to illustrate his own lectures
on design

6 *Salix humilis.*
The low Willow.

7 *Chamæitea, ſiue Salix pumila.*
The dwarfe Willow.

‡ 8 *Salix humilis repens.*
Creeping dwarfe Willow.

which turne into downe that flyeth away with the winde: the root is ſmall and limber, not growing deepe, but running along vpon the vpper cruſt of the earth.

¶ *The Place.*

Theſe Willowes grow in diuers places of England : the Roſe-Willow groweth plentifully in Cambridge ſhire, by the riuers and ditches there in Cambridge towne they grow abundantly about the places called Paradiſe and Hell-mouth, in the way from Cambridge to Grandcheſter : I found the dwarfe Willowes growing neere to a bog or mariſh ground at the further end of Hampſted heath vpon the declining of the hill, in the ditch that incloſeth a ſmall Cottage there, not halfe a furlong from the ſaid houſe or cottage.

¶ *The Time.*

The Willowes doe floure at the beginning of the Spring.

¶ *The Names.*

The Willow tree is called in Greeke ιτια in Latine, *Salix* : in high Dutch, **weyden** : in low Dutch, **wilgen** : in Italian, *Salice* ; *Salcio* : in French, *Saux* : in Spaniſh, *Salguetre*, *Salzer*, and *Sauz* : in Engliſh, Sallow, Withie, and Willow.

78

78   *Gerard's Herbal* A page from Morris's own copy, which he used as a source of information when studying the art of dyeing, and which may well have been a source of pattern ideas also *Courtesy, William Morris Gallery, Walthamstow, Essex*

79   Decorated page from a book of his own poems: written by William Morris for Georgiana Burne-Jones in 1870, exemplifying his early interest in calligraphy and book design *Courtesy, The Victoria and Albert Museum*

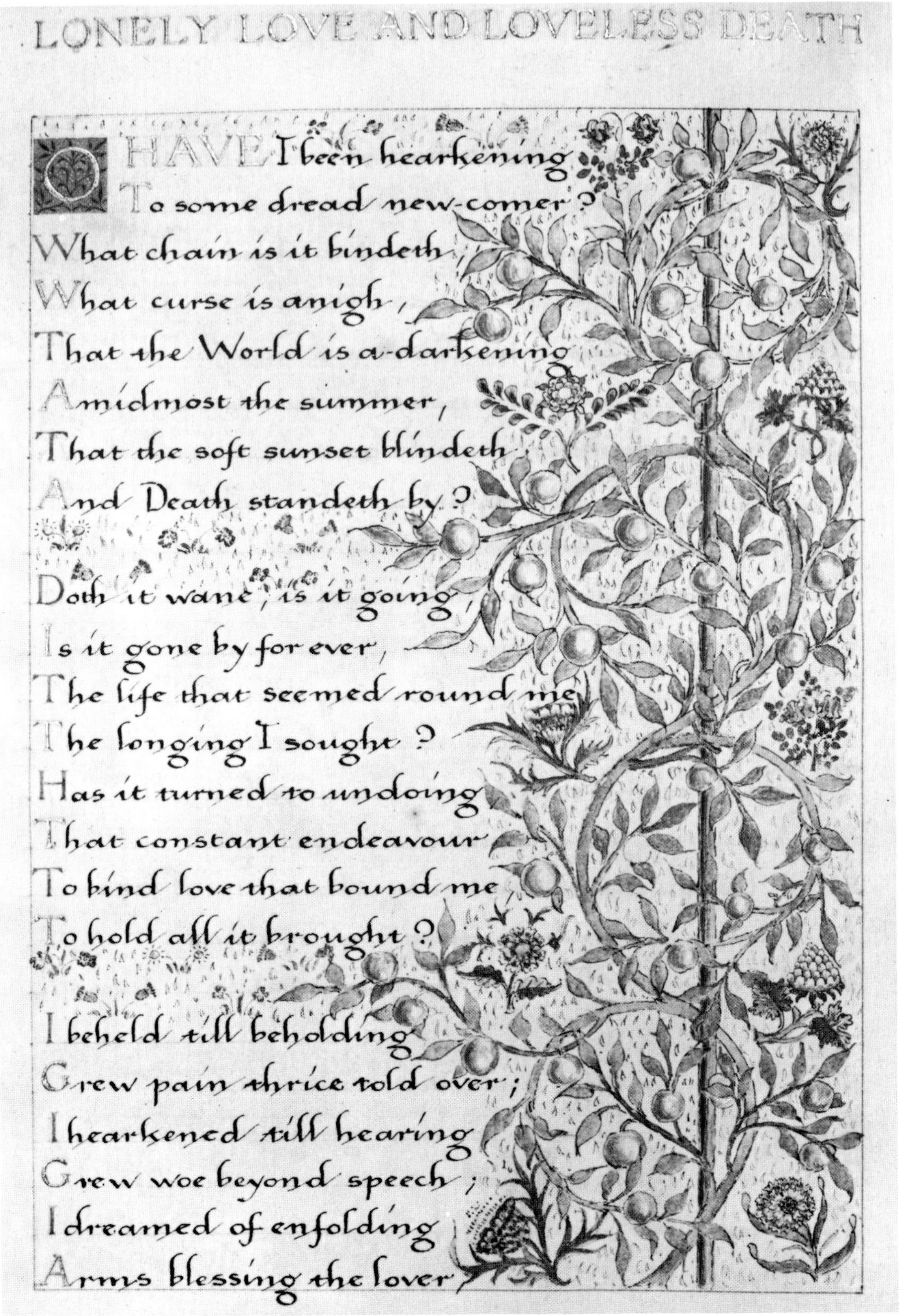

LONELY LOVE AND LOVELESS DEATH

O HAVE I been hearkening
To some dread new-comer?
What chain is it bindeth,
What curse is anigh,
That the World is a-darkening
Amidmost the summer,
That the soft sunset blindeth
And Death standeth by?

Doth it wane, is it going,
Is it gone by for ever,
The life that seemed round me,
The longing I sought?
Has it turned to undoing
That constant endeavour
To bind love that bound me
To hold all it brought?

I beheld till beholding
Grew pain thrice told over;
I hearkened till hearing
Grew woe beyond speech;
I dreamed of enfolding
Arms blessing the lover,

79

That was nat wont to seen the sonne bright;
Ne how the fyr was couched first with stree,
And thanne with drye stokkes, cloven a thre,
And thanne with grene wode and spicerye,
And thanne with clooth of gold, and with perrye,
And gerlandes, hangynge with ful many a flour,
The mirre, thencens, with al so greet odour;
Ne how Arcite lay among al this,
Ne what richesse aboute his body is;
Ne how that Emelye, as was the gyse,
Putte in the fyr of funeral servyse;
Ne how she swowned whan men made fyr,
Ne what she spak, ne what was hir desyr,
Ne what jeweles men in the fyre caste,
Whan that the fyr was greet and brente faste;
Ne how somme caste hir sheeld, & somme hir spere,
And of hire vestiments, whiche that they were,
And coppes ful of wyn, and milk, and blood,
Into the fyr, that brente as it were wood;
Ne how the Grekes, with an huge route,
Thryes they riden al the fyr aboute
Upon the left hand, with a loud shoutynge,
And thryes with hir speres claterynge,
And thryes how the ladyes gonne crye;
And how that lad was homward Emelye;
Ne how Arcite is brent to asshen colde;
Ne how that lyche-wake was yholde
Al thilke nyght; ne how the Grekes pleye
The wake-pleyes; ne kepe I nat to seye
Who wrastleth best naked, with oille enoynt,
Ne who that baar hym best, in no disjoynt.
I wol nat tellen eek how that they goon
Hoom til Atthenes whan the pley is doon;
But shortly to the point thanne wol I wende,
And maken of my longe tale an ende.
BY processe and by lengthe of certeyn yeres,
Al styntyd is the moornynge and the teres.
Of Grekes, by oon general assent
Thanne semed me ther was a parlement
At Atthenes, upon certain poynts and caas;
Among the whiche poynts yspoken was,
To have with certein contrees alliaunce,
And have fully of Thebans obeissaunce.
for which this noble Theseus anon
Leet senden after gentil Palamon,
Unwist of hym what was the cause and why;
But in his blake clothes sorwefully
He cam at his comandement in hye.
Tho sente Theseus for Emelye.
Whan they were set, and hust was al the place,
And Theseus abiden hadde a space
Er any word cam fram his wise brest,
His eyen sette he ther as was his lest,
And with a sad visage he siked stille,
And after that right thus he seyde his wille.
THE firste moevere of the cause above,
Whan he first made the faire cheyne of love,
Greet was theffect, & heigh was his entente;
Wel wiste he why, and what therof he mente;
for with that faire cheyne of love he bond
The fyr, the eyr, the water, and the lond,
In certeyn boundes that they may nat flee.
That same prince, and that moevere, quod he,
Hath stablissed, in this wrecched world adoun,

Certeyne dayes and duracioun
To al that is engendred in this place,
Over the whiche day they may nat pace,
Al mowe they yet tho dayes wel abregge;
Ther nedeth noon auctoritee allegge,
for it is preeved by experience,
But that me list declaren my sentence.
Thanne may men by this ordre wel discerne,
That thilke moevere stable is and eterne.
Wel may men knowe, but it be a fool,
That every part dirryveth from his hool.
for nature hath nat take his bigynnyng
Of no partie ne cantel of a thyng,
But of a thyng that parfit is and stable,
Descendynge so, til it be corrumpable.
And therfore of his wise purveiaunce,
He hath so wel biset his ordinaunce,
That speces of thynges and progressiouns
Shullen enduren by successiouns,
And nat eterne, withouten any lye;
This maystow understonde, and seen at eye.
Loo the ook, that hath so long a norisshynge
from tyme that it first bigynneth sprynge,
And hath so long a lif, as we may see,
Yet at the laste wasted is the tree.
Considereth eek how that the harde stoon
Under oure feet, on which we trede and goon,
Yit wasteth it, as it lyth by the weye;
The brode ryver somtyme wexeth dreye;
The grete toures se we wane and wende;
Thanne may ye se that al this thyng hath ende.
Of man and womman seen we wel also,
That nedeth in oon of thise termes two,
This is to seyn, in youthe or elles age,
He moot be deed, the kyng as shal a page;
Som in his bed, som in the depe see,
Som in the large feeld, as men may se;
Ther helpeth noght, al goth that ilke weye:
Thanne may I seyn that al this thyng moot deye.
What maketh this but Juppiter, the kyng?
The which is prince, and cause of alle thyng,
Convertynge al unto his propre welle,
from which it is dirryved, sooth to telle.
And hereagayns no creature on lyve,
Of no degree, availleth for to stryve.
Thanne is it wysdom, as it thynketh me,
To maken vertu of necessitee,
And take it weel that we may not eschue,
And namely that, that to us alle is due.
And whoso gruccheth ought, he dooth folye,
And rebel is to hym that al may gye;
And certeinly a man hath moost honour,
To dyen in his excellence and flour,
Whan he is siker of his goode name.
Thanne hath he doon his freend ne hym no shame,
And gladder oghte his freend been of his deeth,
Whan with honour upyolden is his breeth,
Than whan his name apalled is for age,
for al forgeten is his vassellage.
Thanne is it best, as for a worthy fame,
To dyen whan that he is best of name.
THE contrarie of al this is wilfulnesse.
Why grucchen we, why have we hevynesse
That good Arcite, of chivalrye the flour,

29

80　Text page from the Kelmscott *Chaucer* completed in 1896. Printed in the Chaucer type (smaller size of Troy) *Courtesy, St Bride's Institute Library*

81　Page from the Kelmscott *Chaucer* with illustration by Burne-Jones. Its decorative borders and initials are all by Morris – over six hundred such designs being produced for the press *Courtesy, St Bride's Institute Library*

Departed is with duetee and honour
Out of this foule prisoun of this lyf?
Why grucchen heere his cosyn and his wyf
Of his welfare that loved hem so weel?
Kan he hem thank? Nay, God woot, never a deel,
That bothe his soule & eek hemself offende,
And yet they mowe hir lustes nat amende.

WHAT may I conclude of this longe serye,
But after wo, I rede us to be merye,
And thanken Juppiter of al his grace?
And er that we departen from this place,
I rede that we make of sorwes two,
O parfit joye, lastynge everemo.
And looketh now, wher moost sorwe is herinne,
Ther wol we first amenden and bigynne.
Suster, quod he, this is my fulle assent,
With all thavys heere of my parlement,
That gentil Palamon, thyn owene knyght,
That serveth yow with wille, herte, and myght,
And evere hath doon, syn that ye first hym knewe,
That ye shul, of your grace, upon hym rewe,
And taken hym for housbonde and for lord;
Lene me youre hond, for this is oure accord.

Lat se now of youre wommanly pitee;
He is a kynges brother sone, pardee,
And though he were a povre bacheler,
Syn he hath served yow so many a yeer
And had for yow so greet adversitee,
It moste been considered, leeveth me,
For gentil mercy oghte to passen right.
THANNE seyde he thus to Palamon ful right:
I trowe ther nedeth litel sermonyng
To make yow assente to this thyng;
Com neer, and taak youre lady by the hond.
Bitwixen hem was maad anon the bond
That highte matrimoigne, or mariage,
By al the conseil and the baronage.
And thus with alle blisse and melodye
Hath Palamon ywedded Emelye;
And God, that al this wyde world hath wroght,
Sende hym his love, that it deere aboght;
For now is Palamon in alle wele,
Lyvynge in blisse, in richesse, and in heele;
And Emelye hym loveth so tendrely,
And he hire serveth al so gentilly,
That nevere was ther no word hem bitwene
Of jalousie, or any oother tene.
Thus endeth Palamon and Emelye,
And God save al this faire compaignye,
Heere is ended the Knyghtes Tale

82 Designs by Burne-Jones for the projected
Earthly Paradise of 1867–8 engraved by William
Morris *Courtesy, William Morris Gallery,
Walthamstow, Essex*

83 Trial pull of type and decoration for the
projected illustrated edition of *Love is Enough*
1870–1 by William Morris and Burne-Jones.
Printed at the Chiswick Press, using Basle type
*Courtesy, William Morris Gallery, Walthamstow,
Essex*

Love is Enough.

LOVE is enough: though the world
    be a-waning,
And the woods have no voice but
    the voice of complaining;
Though the sky be too dark for
    dim eyes to discover
The gold-cups and daisies fair
    blooming thereunder,
Though the hill be held shadows,
    and the sea a dark wonder,
And this day draw a veil over all deeds passed over,
Yet their hands shall not tremble, their feet shall not falter;
The void shall not weary, the fear shall not alter
These lips and these eyes of the loved and the lover.

THE EMPEROR.

The spears flashed by me, and the spears swept round,
And in war's hopeless tangle was I bound,
But straw and stubble were the cold points found,
For still thy hands led down the weary way.

THE EMPRESS.

Through hall and street they led me as a queen,
They looked to see me proud and cold of mien,
I heeded not though all my tears were seen,
For still I dreamed of thee throughout the day.

THE EMPEROR.

Wild over bow and bulwark swept the sea
Unto the iron coast upon our lee,
Like painted cloth its fury was to me,
For still thy hands led down the weary way.

3

A TALE OF THE HOUSE OF THE WOLFINGS AND ALL THE KINDREDS OF THE MARK WRITTEN IN PROSE AND IN VERSE BY WILLIAM MORRIS.

WHILES IN THE EARLY WINTER EVE
WE PASS AMID THE GATHERING NIGHT
SOME HOMESTEAD THAT WE HAD TO LEAVE
YEARS PAST ; AND SEE ITS CANDLES BRIGHT
SHINE IN THE ROOM BESIDE THE DOOR
WHERE WE WERE MERRY YEARS AGONE
BUT NOW MUST NEVER ENTER MORE,
AS STILL THE DARK ROAD DRIVES US ON.
E'EN SO THE WORLD OF MEN MAY TURN
AT EVEN OF SOME HURRIED DAY
AND SEE THE ANCIENT GLIMMER BURN
ACROSS THE WASTE THAT HATH NO WAY ;
THEN WITH THAT FAINT LIGHT IN ITS EYES
A WHILE I BID IT LINGER NEAR
AND NURSE IN WAVERING MEMORIES
THE BITTER-SWEET OF DAYS THAT WERE.

LONDON 1889: REEVES AND TURNER 196 STRAND.

84   Title-page *The House of the Wolfings* designed
by Morris, printed at the Chiswick Press
November–December 1888 *Photo W V Whittaker*

Now came an ancient warrior into the space between the men and the wild-wood holding in his hand a kindled torch; and first he faced due south by the sun, then, turning, he slowly paced the whole circle going from east to west, and so on till he had reached the place he started from: then he dashed the torch to the ground and quenched the fire, and so went his ways to his own company again.

Then the old Dayling warrior on the mound-top drew his sword, and waved it flashing in the sun toward the four quarters of the heavens; and thereafter blew again a blast on the War-horn. Then fell utter silence on the whole assembly, and the wood was still around them, save here and there the stamping of a war-horse or the sound of his tugging at the woodland grass; for there was little resort of birds to the depths of the thicket, and the summer morning was windless.

CHAPTER VIII.

THE FOLK-MOTE OF THE MARKMEN.

SO the Dayling warrior lifted up his voice and said:

"O kindreds of the Markmen, hearken the words I say;
For no chancehap assembly is gathered here to-day.
The fire hath gone around us in the hands of our very kin,
And twice the horn hath sounded, and the Thing is hallowed in.
Will ye hear or forbear to hearken the tale there is to tell?
There are many mouths to tell it, and a many know it well.
And the tale is this, that the foemen against our kindreds fare
Who eat the meadows desert, and burn the desert bare."

Then sat he down on the turf seat; but there arose a murmur in the assembly as of men eager to hearken; and without more ado came a man out of a company of the Upper-mark, and clomb up to the top of the Speech-Hill, and spoke in a loud voice:

85   Text page of *The House of the Wolfings*, set in
the Basle type *Photo W V Whittaker*

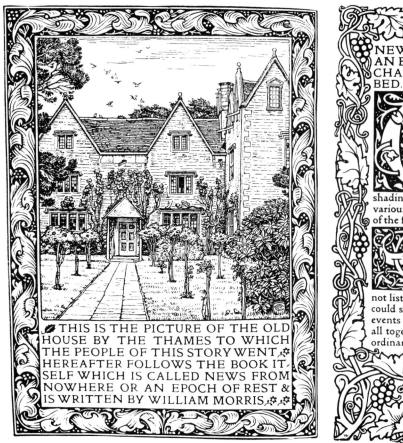

THIS IS THE PICTURE OF THE OLD HOUSE BY THE THAMES TO WHICH THE PEOPLE OF THIS STORY WENT. HEREAFTER FOLLOWS THE BOOK IT SELF WHICH IS CALLED NEWS FROM NOWHERE OR AN EPOCH OF REST & IS WRITTEN BY WILLIAM MORRIS.

NEWS FROM NOWHERE OR AN EPOCH OF REST. CHAPTER I. DISCUSSION AND BED.

UP at the League, says a friend, there had been one night a brisk conversational discussion, as to what would happen on the Morrow of the Revolution, finally shading off into a vigorous statement by various friends, of their views on the future of the fully-developed new society.

SAYS our friend: Considering the subject, the discussion was good-tempered; for those present, being used to public meetings & after-lecture debates, if they did not listen to each other's opinions, which could scarcely be expected of them, at all events did not always attempt to speak all together, as is the custom of people in ordinary polite society when conversing

86 Frontispiece and opening of text of *News From Nowhere*, Kelmscott Press, 1892 (issued March 1893). The text set in the Golden type. The frontispiece is a picture of Kelmscott Manor
Photo W V Whittaker

driven to it I would almost sacrifice out-door space to it. Then, of course, there is the ornament, which, as we must all allow, may easily be over-done in mere living-houses, but can hardly be in mote-halls and markets, and so forth. I must tell you, though, that my great-grandfather some-times tells me I am a little cracked on this subject of fine building; and indeed I do think that the energies of mankind are chiefly of use to them for such work; for in that direction I can see no end to the work, while in many others a limit does seem possible."

CHAPTER VI. A LITTLE SHOPPING.

 S he spoke, we came sud-denly out of the wood-land into a short street of handsomely built houses which my companion named to me at once as Piccadilly: the lower part of these I should have called shops, if it had not been that, as far as I could see, the people were ignorant of the arts of buying and selling. Wares were displayed in their finely designed fronts, as if to tempt people in, & people stood and looked at them, or went in and came out with parcels under their arms just like the real thing. On each side of the street ran an elegant

46

arcade to protect foot-passengers, as in some of the old Italian cities. About half-way down, a huge building of the kind I was now prepared to expect told me that this also was a centre of some kind, and had its special public buildings. ¶ Said Dick: "Here, you see, is another market on a dif-ferent plan from most others: the upper stories of these houses are used for guest-houses; for people from all about the country are apt to drift up hither from time to time, as folk are very thick upon the ground, which you will see evidence of presently, & there are people who are fond of crowds, though I can't say that I am." ¶ I couldn't help smiling to see how long a tradition would last. Here was the ghost of London still asserting itself as a centre, an intellectual centre, for aught I knew. How-ever, I said nothing, except that I asked him to drive very slowly, as the things in the booths looked exceedingly pretty. "Yes," said he, "this is a very good market for pretty things, & is mostly kept for the handsomer goods, as the Houses-of-Parliament market, where they set out cabbages and turnips and such like things, along with beer and the rougher kind of wine, is so near." ¶ Then he looked at me curiously, & said, "Perhaps you would like to do a little shopping, as 'tis called." I looked at what I could see of my rough blue duds, which I had plenty of opportunity of contrasting with the gay attire of the citizens we had come across; and I thought that if, as seemed likely, I

47

87 Text pages of the Kelmscott Press *News From Nowhere*, set in the Golden type *Photo W V Whittaker*

HERE END THE TREATISES OF BENVENUTO CELLINI
ON METAL WORK AND SCULPTURE, MADE INTO ENG-
LISH FROM THE ITALIAN OF THE MARCIAN CODEX BY
C. R. ASHBEE, AND PRINTED BY HIM AT THE GUILD'S
PRESS AT ESSEX HOUSE, WITH THE ASSISTANCE OF
LAURENCE HODSON WHO SOUGHT TO KEEP LIVING
THE TRADITIONS OF GOOD PRINTING REFOUNDED BY
WILLIAM MORRIS, THE MASTER CRAFTSMAN, AND
LIKEWISE OF T. BINNING & J. TIPPETT, COMPOSITORS,
AND S. MOWLEM, PRESSMAN, WHO CAME TO ESSEX
HOUSE FROM THE KELMSCOTT PRESS TO THAT END.
BEGUN APRIL, 1898; FINISHED OCTOBER, 1898,

Published by EDWARD ARNOLD, 37 Bedford
Street, Strand; and of the 600 copies printed,
this copy is No. 557

88   *Colophon of the Treatise on Goldsmithing* by
Benvenuto Cellini, translated by C R Ashbee and
printed at his Essex House Press
Photo W V Whittaker

TWENTY-ONE YEARS AGO IN THIS ROOM then filled with looms, William Morris began the manufacture of his famous Hammersmith carpets. For many years thereafter it was in regular use for Socialist meetings and chiefly and exclusively at last for those of the Hammersmith Socialist Society. This Society, the last of those founded or joined by Morris, represents in a sense the success and failure of his life. It certainly represents the subject which in those later years engrossed his mind and lay nearest to his heart. When, therefore, Mrs. Cobden-Sanderson, one of the friends for whom Morris had a very special affection, asked me to open, in this historic room, this winter's course of meetings of the Hammersmith Socialist Society—the first after long disuse—with an address on the founder of the Society, and the former master of the house, the invitation was one which I could not well decline on the ground I have given elsewhere, that what I have to say about Morris I have already said in the published record of his life. ⁅ I do not propose, however, now to go beyond or vary from that record, or to diverge into general criticism. What we think of great men matters very much to ourselves individually. It matters little to others; & least of all to the great men themselves, who were not much affected by criticism when they lived, & whose influence upon the world is hardly touched by the criticism, even though that be fairer in its judgment and larger in its view, which follows them after death. For this reason I will not attempt to give any general

I

89   *Address* by J W Mackail on the occasion of the resumption of the meetings of the Hammersmith Socialist Society at Kelmscott House, November 1900. Printed by Cobden-Sanderson and Emery Walker at their Doves Press, April 1900

90

90   Morris's Kelmscott mark, used as a colophon
in most of the books issued from the press